SOUNDINGS

# SOUNDINGS

## *A Thematic Guide*
## *for Daily Scripture Prayer*

---

# Rev. Chris Aridas

IMAGE BOOKS
A Division of
Doubleday & Company, Inc.
GARDEN CITY, NEW YORK
1984

Library of Congress Cataloging in Publication Data
Aridas, Chris, 1947–
    Food for the journey.
    1. Meditations.   2. Devotional calendars—Catholic
Church.   3. Catholic Church—Prayer-books and devotions—
English.   I. Title.
BX2182.2.A74   1984            242′.2            83–16509

ISBN: 0-385-19157-X

# Contents

# Contents

# Preface

I firmly believe that books on prayer are usually a diversion rather than a help to the pray-er. The individual spends hours poring over a methodology of prayer rather than allowing himself/herself the quiet time needed to allow the Spirit the opportunity to pray within. When asked to write a book of daily scripture meditations, therefore, I was quite hesitant, knowing from experience that the Lord does not operate in such a neat fashion. More often than not, I am led to spend many days with one particular passage of scripture, seeking to hear clearly his voice speaking within. Changing the passage every day does not usually give me the time to hear what the Spirit might be saying to me. Perhaps the same is true for you.

When I explained this to the editors, they agreed to the present format. It was a helpful compromise which gives the reader a freedom to choose a different passage every day of the year, or to stay with a particular theme for as long as the Spirit directs. In providing both options, each person will be able to move at his/her own rate, following his/her own path as each is led by the Spirit of God.

The book, therefore, has been divided into three sections. The first, which includes the Introduction and a brief chapter on the importance of scripture prayer is meant to set the stage. It is not a detailed analysis of prayer, but an introduction to the scripture themes which follow. The second section includes the themes themselves. They are not arranged in a particular order, and can be chosen at random. Please do not feel obliged to take

Theme 1 and follow through, week by week, to Theme 52. Though you can use the book that way, it is not necessary to do so. Let the Lord guide you. The final section of Appendixes offers a more detailed explanation of scripture prayer for those who are interested, as well as an explanation of the individual's psychological and spiritual growth patterns. There are also several reference sections which might be helpful when you are looking for a particular passage.

At this time, I would like to thank the many people who supported me in this effort, especially those with whom I live or work. They were especially patient during the times I could think of nothing but "the book"; their encouragement was a joy. A special word of thanks to Tom Heller for allowing me to use his story, A Parable. I have told it many times, and "rewritten" it more than once, yet it remains his. And finally, the men and women who, while guiding me on my journey of faith, have lovingly taught me how to hear the Lord. To them this book is dedicated: Msgr. Peter Chiara, Sr. Thelma Hall, Sr. Brendan McQuillan, and Fr. James Wheeler.

# A Parable: The Call to Journey

Two friends, seeking a better place to live, set out on a journey. After many adventures, and a great deal of traveling, they came to the edge of a thick, deep forest which seemed to stretch toward infinity. Here they had to choose one of two possible directions: to settle at the edge of the forest, or continue through the dark passage ahead of them trusting that their dream lay beyond. Realizing that they were too tired to make this important decision, they resolved to rest, and discuss the possibilities in the morning. Wearied from their journey, and excited about their next adventure, they retired for the evening.

During the night, both men were blessed with a powerful and vivid dream. From a silence deep within, a voice spoke clearly to each: "Go through the forest; take the path prepared for you. I will be there to protect and guide you. Your dream awaits you —brighter and more pleasing than you ever imagined. The road might seem difficult, but I will be your guide." Then, just as suddenly as it had come, the warm, comforting presence of the voice left, and each fell into a deep sleep.

The next morning, the friends hastened to share the strange and wonderful happenings of the night before. Each took great confidence in the confirming experience of his friend—yet looked hesitantly toward the dark forest ahead. Finally, one of them spoke firmly: "Let us take the path. Our desire is to seek a new home, so let us continue trusting the voice we have heard. We will be protected; the voice promised us. Did we both not feel deep within us the power of its words? I believe only Truth can have such power."

But the other was afraid. "Perhaps we have been traveling too long," he said, "or part of us simply longs for adventure, moving us to continue, heedless of the dangers and the darkness ahead. In the light of the morning the forest looks bleak and unfriendly. What will it be like when we are within its embrace later on this evening? Why don't we camp here, and make our home amidst the trees by the forest's edge. I'm sure this place can be quite comfortable."

But the first man could not forget the words he had heard the evening before. They debated the entire morning, but neither was convinced by the other's argument. So, sadly, the friends took leave of each other. One, guided by the words spoken in the dream, left and began the long and difficult journey through the forest, while the other remained and built a place for himself in its shadow.

At first, the man who lived by the edge of the woods enjoyed relative ease, disturbed by only two difficulties. First, for a long time, he could not shake the reality of the voice which spoke to him in his dream; nor could he ignore the confidence with which he first received the words spoken. In addition, the image of his friend continued to accompany that voice, and disturbed both his conscious and sleeping moments.

Secondly, he grew uncomfortable with the nearness of the forest. In building his home, he had been too busy to hear the strange sounds, or see the dark shadows that sprang from the woods. Now that he was settled, however, they filled him with fear. He began to lock his house, and spent a great deal of time devising techniques and machineries of defense, lest he be bothered by any strange forms of life coming from the darkness at his doorstep. Each night, therefore, it took him longer and longer to calm his fear so that he might fall asleep. But each night also took him farther and farther from the memory of his friend, and the words of guidance spoken to him on the night of his dream. Soon, he forgot these altogether and was left with only his fear. But it was great enough to occupy all his energy. And so he passed his days.

The second man also feared the sounds and the darkness of the forest. At first, moreover, he did not hear the comforting voice all that day, or the next. Yet, he continued, motivated by the promise he had received the night the voice echoed within his being.

As he continued his journey, however, he began to notice a change. He learned to "see" in the darkness, and to recognize more quickly those forest spaces which could provide him with food and shelter. Most important, however, he learned to hear and trust in the reality and the guidance of the voice. Some nights when he went to sleep he would "hear" a new word, or feel once again the warm, comforting presence which motivated his initial steps toward the forest. In many ways his life was not as comfortable as that of his friend who lived at the edge of the forest, but he grew hardier and wiser, confident and peaceful as he continued the journey.

Finally, at the end of his life, he reached the land beyond the woods. By that time, however, he had grown to love the bleakest forest passages through which he had journeyed; he had grown to love the moments of silence when he listened intently in the dark hoping to hear a new word, or receive a further direction; he had learned to know and love what seemed to be difficult, because he had learned to know and love the voice speaking within.

\* \* \*

In the parable above, who are you? Can you identify with either or both characters? Probably so, since we have all taken a journey in one way or another. It is part of our very experience, whether we be the businessperson commuting to work, the executive flying from one appointment to another, the parent packing bottles, diapers, and baby toys in order to go food shopping, or the child who, waving goodbye to the parent anxiously gazing out the window, walks two blocks—or two miles—to school.

Regardless of the type of journey we make, however, there are several characteristics which are common to all: listening and seeing. We need to *listen* to directions, and *look* for signs that those directions are being followed. This is true in every case, even those journeys that are made in silence or in secret. Then, however, the directions to which we "listen" are those that have been planted in our heart, thereby echoing within, and the signs that we "see" are those which touch our inner affections.

It should not take us by surprise, therefore, that God would use this common human experience as a means of communicating to us. As scripture says, ". . . the Word is very near to you, it is in your mouth and in your heart for your observance" (Dt. 30:143). In fact, the journey-image is key in understanding how God spoke to his people, and drew them into his presence.

Starting with Abraham who heard the call and obeyed: "Yahweh said to Abram, 'Leave your country, your family, and your father's house, for the land I will show you. I will make you a great nation; I will bless you and make your name so famous that it will be used as a blessing.' " (Gn. 12:1–2); and culminating in the Exodus account of Israel's journey to the Promised Land we see the journey-image used again and again, both in the Old and New Testament: Elijah's journey to Mount Horeb, Jonah's journey to Nineveh, Mary's journey to Elizabeth, Jesus's journey to Jerusalem. In each example, the characteristics of listening and seeing remain the same.

Another characteristic of the journeys mentioned above is that the people on them often did not understand or know where they were going. Abraham, for example, had no idea where the Promised Land was; he only knew and trusted the inner voice of God speaking to his heart. The people of Israel, led by Moses, journeyed forty years before they reached the land promised to them when they were held captive by Pharaoh. They journeyed, in a sense, to a land they could not see, except with the eyes of faith, and were guided by a voice they could not "hear," except that it was spoken to Moses within the depths of his being. And finally, the man in our parable, "sensed" his heart's desire was a new land, and proceeded, with no visible direction, toward his goal.

And so it is with us. We too are called to make a journey, to enter the darkened forest and be guided by the voice echoing within. Like the man in the parable, we are called to proceed with confidence, listening for God's voice, so we may recognize the signs that confirm the reality of his words to us. And so we pray.

In the chapter that follows, one way of listening to God's voice is described, followed by themes and meditations which may assist you in recognizing the voice when it speaks. In doing so you will receive strength, guidance, and encouragement as you continue your journey to the Father.

# CHAPTER ONE

## *Sacred Scripture: Our Way to Listen*

Like our human experience, prayer is a journey: a journey through the very center of our being, where we can "listen" to the stillness of the Spirit's voice, and "see" the majesty of the Father present within. As in human experiences where each journey is different, so with our prayer. Your experience and my experience will not be the same, although similarities may abound.

As Christian pray-ers, therefore, we need to discover our own way, our own rhythm, remembering, of course, that the Lord's way is the guideline we follow—the way of death/resurrection. How I am led on this journey, therefore, depends very much on what I offer: my time, my availability to the power of the Spirit, my willingness to abide in the Father's will, my singlehearted-ness. Our seriousness about this journey is shown very clearly by the priority given to it: how much time I offer, what quality of time is offered, and what is done during the time offered.

On this inner journey, therefore, the important thing to remember is not the *act* of prayer itself, but the relationship that is meant to develop with the Lord Jesus—a relationship that enables us to "hear" and "see" clearly. It would be helpful, therefore, if we consciously and continuously checked our motivations for praying. Am I doing it because it makes me feel good? Or because I will experience God's presence? Or because I am afraid of getting God angry? Should these, or similar responses, be ours, we may be "hearing" and "seeking" ourself and our own gratification rather than the abiding will of the Father who desires we receive completely the sonship/daughtership offered us in his Son, Jesus. But do not get discouraged.

Our motivations are not expected to be "pure" at the very beginning. If we are faithful, God's cleansing power will bring the process to completion.

As faith, hope, and charity are gifts of God, so too with prayer. He alone gives us the gift. We, however, can prepare for receiving the gift by our fervently asking, and by willingly dying to self. Through it all, however, it is the Lord who really does the work.

"Yes" is therefore the real prayer. "Yes" to all that is done by him, for me; "yes" to all he desires to give; "yes" to his love poured out in Jesus. "Yes" to a deliberate recalling to mind his holy presence, and spending time there. "Yes" to listening to the word echoing within, the reality of love offered, the Life poured out for us to embrace.

In listening to God's word, therefore, be assured that he will speak—indeed that he has already spoken; that he has already communicated himself to us in the fullness of life, Jesus Christ, his Word made flesh: "At various times in the past and in various different ways, God spoke to our ancestors through the prophets; but in our own time, the last days, he has spoken to us through his Son" (Heb. 1:1–2).

There are no difficult "requirements" for hearing this word, except the exhortation of John, speaking of Jesus, who says, "If you make my word your home you will indeed be my disciples, you will learn the truth and the truth will make you free" (Jn. 8:31b–32). For the words of God, "expressed in human language, have been made like human discourse, just as of old the Word of the eternal Father, when he took to himself the weak flesh of humanity, became like other men" *(Dogmatic Constitution on Divine Revelation,* 13).

Through our "obedience of faith" (Rm. 16:26), therefore, an obedience by which we willingly entrust ourselves to God, offering complete submission of mind and heart to him, we grow in the inner attitude needed to hear the Word spoken in the sacred text.

By being personally present to the Word in scripture, we are now empowered to listen and speak to the Lord. For the word is indeed the power of God for the salvation of all who believe (cf. Rm. 1:16) spoken to us, and enfleshed for us so we may become familiar with our Savior and Lover. In the words of St. Jerome: "Ignorance of scripture is ignorance of Christ."

When I pray, therefore, it is because I have faith in Jesus Christ, a faith which hears and responds to the voice of the Spirit speaking through the sacred text, the Word of God, where the Father of all meets his children. Faith, then, is my stance in the world, my decision to perceive reality in a particular way—the way of Jesus's death and resurrection. It is my willingness to allow the Holy Spirit to hover over the chaos of my mind and heart, as he hovered over creation, speaking a word of harmony and order.

And I am able to pray, therefore, because God gives me the eyes to see—to see his waiting patiently for me, waiting for me to welcome him and receive him with and in my entire being; and the ears to hear—to hear his voice speaking a word of love eternal, speaking in every way possible so I might respond. These eyes and ears of faith are, of course, really Jesus's, since it is through him we have in the Spirit our way to the Father.

In prayer, therefore, we are in the Son, and it is the Son in us who loves the Father through the Spirit. This is why we say it is God's action, the action of Trinity—Father, Son, and Spirit— joining us in the constant exchange of love that is reality itself.

And so we prepare ourselves in emptiness, asking the Spirit to grant us a listening heart that will receive all the Father offers. Even here it is God's action transforming us, hoeing us, pruning us. What is our part? Simply to let him, and to unite our will with his Son, whose "power to save is utterly certain, since he is living for ever to intercede for all who come to God through him" (Heb. 7:25).

Jesus, therefore, is the one teacher of prayer: Jesus who acts in and through the Spirit. Our prayer is his, the prayer of the Son ceaselessly addressing the Father, "Abba," in the power of the Spirit. It is for us to accept, and open an inner space for Jesus praying within, so that sharing his suffering we might share in his glory. As mentioned previously, the "suffering" we share is our dying to self, our being emptied, our accepting the limitation of having nothing to return to the One who offers us everything.

At the heart of our prayer, then, is the mystery of Jesus's death and resurrection. We are called to live this mystery in the events that are interwoven within our existence, through our dying and rising in daily life. This *process* is further explained in Appendix A for those who are interested in a more detailed presentation.

In Appendix B, I have given two ways that a person might pray with scripture. The first is an exercise in imaginative prayer; the second is an exercise in dialogue prayer. Neither way is better than the other, nor are they the only ways available. They are offered simply for your reference, should you require further direction.

As with any prayer experience, we must find our rhythm and stick to it. In finding this rhythm, the following guidelines might be helpful:

1. Have a set time. Thinking that the time will "appear" without planning is a foolish approach. As in all relationships, time must be allotted so the relationship can develop. I find, for example, that I need to decide the night before when I will pray on the following day; others, however, are able to lock into a set time which seldom varies. Regardless of how the time gets scheduled, be sure to schedule it. Remember also that when the time is offered is indicative of the priority given to developing

this relationship with the Lord. Avoid, therefore, scheduling a time when you are unable to function physically. I would find it impossible, for example, to pray at midnight, although there are some people for whom this is their best time. Find your rhythm, and stick to it.

2. It is often helpful to have a place to pray—a place where you can be alone, and quiet. A place that is "special" in some way: perhaps a Bible enthroned, or a candle lit, or a "prayer chair." In other words, a place that has a sacred meaning to you, so that going there you can wait expectantly for the Lord.

Some people, of course, may find it very difficult to have such a place. Their living quarters or working area simply does not allow for this luxury; perhaps even their parish church is closed during the hours they have allotted for prayer. For all of us, however, the heart, in some way, becomes that place. Thus we are never limited to the availability of certain structures.

3. Do not worry about distractions. They are part and parcel of everyone's prayer experience. Each time they occur, simply remember that every distraction gives you another opportunity to choose the Lord in prayer! In many ways they are like puppies who continually jump at your feet while you are trying to do something. If you keep pushing the puppies away, they will keep coming back with renewed vigor. If you ignore them, however, they will undoubtedly go away or calm down. The same is true with distractions.

4. Do not be concerned with accomplishing anything during prayer. Prayer is God's gift to us, which we are called to offer back to him. There is nothing for us to accomplish. In fact, the "quality" of our prayer depends on our openness and purity of heart, not the number of thoughts we had, or images received.

5. Be patient. Our goal is to be in Jesus. This involves the lifelong process of dying to self and rising to him. It does not happen in a moment; it takes a lifetime.

# CHAPTER TWO
## *Themes and Meditations*

In this section, various themes and reflections have been provided for your prayer experience. The emphasis, of course, is on the scripture selections that have been chosen. Note that the brief reflection which begins each theme is not meant to be the subject of the meditation itself, but a possible direction or idea which might be helpful.

It must also be emphasized that a new theme need not be started each week. The pray-er should remain with one theme for as long as the Spirit speaks to him/her. Only then should a new one be chosen. The Lord himself will tell you (through your experience) what the next theme should be.

For each theme, ten passages from scripture have been selected, thereby presenting a cross section from the entire scripture corpus. Having settled on a particular theme, scan through the scripture selections listed; they have been "summarized" to give a general idea of the passages' content. Be sure to use the entire scripture passage when you pray, since the summary is only that, a summary. This is especially true of the miracle accounts, and the longer sections from St. John where space did not permit the entire reference to be quoted. For all the passages, the Jerusalem Bible translation has been utilized.

# BE STILL AND KNOW THAT
# I AM GOD

Here's where the growth takes place—in silence. It is here, within, that a fertile field is hoed; where God's Word can take root, spreading its life-giving branches into every nook and cranny of our lives. It is here, in silence, where the voice of God can be heard echoing loudly for us to hear and respond. Here in silence.

From the very beginning we sense that this is no easy task. More than likely we are afraid of the silence: afraid of what the Lord might ask; afraid of what he might reveal; afraid we will hear nothing. Yet, despite such fears, it remains essential that we strive, as best as we are able, to create that silent place in our lives. For some, it's a special room or chair; for others, a special time of day. Regardless, we need the silence to hear the Lord's voice echoing within.

During this time, do not be afraid of turning off the radio or TV, of taking the telephone off the hook, of asking your spouse or family members to leave you alone for a while. Tell them why. You will discover that the fears have disappeared once you have chosen the silent space in which the Lord speaks his words of love. Such a decision and choice is always rewarded with a listening heart.

## Scripture Verses

Be quiet before Yahweh, and wait patiently for him. (Ps. 37:7)

It is good to wait in silence
    for Yahweh to save . . .
to sit in solitude and silence
    when the Lord fastens it on him. (Lm. 3:26–28)

Keep silence before me,
let the people renew their strength. (Is. 41:1)

As for Mary, she treasured these things, and pondered them in her heart. (Lk. 2:19)

[Martha] You worry and fret about so many things, and yet few are needed, indeed only one. It is Mary who has chosen the better part. (Lk. 10:41–42)

[Elijah] went into the cave and spent the night in it . . . Then Yahweh himself went by . . . not in the wind . . . not in the earthquake . . . not in the fire. And after the fire there came the sound of a gentle breeze. (1 Kg. 19:9–12)

Stand firm, and you will see what Yahweh will do to save you today; . . . you have only to keep still. (Ex. 14:13–14)

———❦———

## *For Further Reflection*

But Yahweh is in his holy Temple:
let the whole earth be silent before him. (Hab. 2:20)

Let all mankind be silent before Yahweh!
For he is awakening and is coming from his holy dwelling.
(Zc. 2:17)

For thus says the Lord Yahweh, the Holy One of Israel:
Your salvation lay in conversion and tranquillity,
your strength, in complete trust. (Is. 30:15)

# 2

## GOD'S INVITATION

One of the greatest difficulties encountered in accepting the Lord's invitation is one of pride, for we have convinced ourselves that we can do anything and everything on our own—including coming to the Lord. But as the songwriter says, "It ain't necessarily so." In fact, without humbly *accepting* God's invitation, we will never come to know him.

This acceptance is not automatic; it requires a decision, a choosing. More often than not, however, we say that the invitation has been accepted, when in reality we have stored it away, unopened, oblivious to its contents, like a wedding invitation that has been placed, unopened, in the closet. Has such an invitation really been accepted? Has it really been received, or responded to, with the heart?

God's invitation is first and foremost an invitation to accept him as Lord and Creator, by acknowledging ourselves as the saved and the creature. Such a stance is not too popular in our contemporary culture which emphasizes independence and self-reliance. Yet the invitation remains. Will we come, acknowledging our empty-handedness, so that we can be filled to overflowing by him who wants "everyone to be saved and reach full knowledge of the truth"?

## Scripture Verses

Come to me, all you who labor and are overburdened, and I will give you rest. Shoulder my yoke and learn from me, for I am gentle and humble of heart, and you will find rest for your souls. (Mt. 11:28–29)

Oh, come to the water all you who are thirsty;
though you have no money, come!
Buy corn without money, and eat,
and, at no cost, wine and milk. (Is. 55:1)

[Jesus] wants everyone to be saved and reach full knowledge of the truth. (1 Tm. 2:4)

Look, I am standing at the door knocking. If one of you hears me calling and opens the door, I will come in to share his meal, side by side with him. (Rv. 3:20)

The Spirit and the Bride say, "Come." Let everyone who listens answer, "Come." Then let all who are thirsty come: all who want it may have the water of life, and have it free. (Rv. 22:17)

"Lord," he [Peter] said "if it is you, tell me to come to you across the water." "Come" said Jesus. (Mt. 14:28)

*The Call of the Disciples*
[Jesus said] Follow me. (Mk. 10:17–22)

## For Further Reflection

Let the little children come to me; . . . for it is to such as these that the kingdom of God belongs. (Mk. 10:14)

[The King said] the wedding is ready; but as those who were invited proved to be unworthy, go to the crossroads in the town and invite everyone you can find to the wedding. *(See* Mt. 22:1–11)

[Jesus] is the living stone, . . . set yourselves close to him so that you too, the holy priesthood that offers the spiritual sacrifices which Jesus Christ has made acceptable to God, may be living stones making a spiritual house. (1 Pt. 2:4–5)

# 3

# GOD OFFERS FORGIVENESS

The key to receiving God's forgiveness is to come back to him as quickly as possible! It is not that our delaying tempts him to cease forgiving, but rather it makes it more difficult for us to trust in his constant and never changing love.

It is no secret that sin hampers our ability to see the Lord by causing us to feel disoriented, murky, and sluggish. Rationalizations abound, and prayer probably dries up and ceases. Sin convinces us that our food is other than the Lord; that our breath is other than his Spirit; that our heart's desire is other than the Father. And so we stay away because all seems dark.

Yet his call remains constant: "Come back to me with all your heart." Should you begin to feel the effects of sin, do not delay. Return to him immediately. A simple prayer of the heart will be helpful in piercing through the darkness and gaining us freedom. The Sacrament of Reconciliation is also a powerful opportunity to know his forgiving love. Do not delay. Each moment apart from the reality of his love is a moment outside of reality itself.

## Scripture Verses

It is not those who are well that need the doctor, but the sick. I have not come to call the virtuous, but sinners to repentance. (Lk. 5:31–32)

But now, now—it is Yahweh who speaks—
come back to me with all your heart,
fasting, weeping, mourning.
Let your hearts be broken, not your garments torn,
turn to Yahweh your God again,
for he is all tenderness and compassion,
slow to anger, rich in graciousness,
and ready to relent. (Jl. 2:12–13)

There will be more rejoicing in heaven over one repentant sinner than over ninety-nine virtuous men who have no need of
repentance. *(See Lk. 15:4–7)*

*Parable of the Forgiving Father*
    While he was still a long way off, his father saw him and was
moved to pity. He ran to the boy, clasped him in his arms and
kissed him tenderly. (Lk. 15:11–32)

If anyone should sin,
we have our advocate with the Father,
Jesus Christ, who is just;
he is the sacrifice that takes our sins away,
and not only ours,
but the whole world's. (1 Jn. 2:1–2)

If you never overlooked our sins, Yahweh,
Lord, could anyone survive?
But you do forgive us:
and for that we revere you. (Ps. 130:3–4)

I said, "I will go to Yahweh
and confess my fault."
And you, you have forgiven the wrong I did,
have pardoned my sin. (Ps. 32:5)

———————&ni;———————

## *For Further Reflection*

You will not scorn this crushed and broken heart. *(See* Ps. 51)

He who conceals his faults will not prosper,
he who confesses and renounces them will find
mercy. (Pr. 28:13)

God who is faithful and just
will forgive our sins and purify us
from everything that is wrong. (1 Jn. 1:9)

# 4

# CHOSEN BY GOD

To be chosen is to be set aside for a special purpose. It implies that other choices could have been made but were not; that other options were available but the one chosen was the one most desired. This is what it means to be chosen by God. For some reason, which only love can identify, humankind was chosen to bear within its very frame the image of the Creator. We were chosen to be mirrors of the Light, bearers of the Word, temples of the Spirit.

Why such an honor? Love knows. Certainly not because of our power, or ability, or receptivity. Those are far too frail and limited to warrant such an honor. But then, perhaps that is precisely why we were chosen: We are frail, we are limited, and God wanted all to see how unique and unilateral his love is.

Regardless, the fact remains. We are the chosen ones of God —those who have been given the privilege of proclaiming all that he has done for us who are unworthy.

## Scripture Verses

You did not choose me,
no, I chose you . . .
to go out and to bear fruit. (Jn. 15:16)

Like shoots of wild olive, you have been grafted among the rest to share with them the rich sap provided by the olive tree itself, but still . . . remember that you do not support the root; it is the root that supports you. (Rm. 11:17–18)

You have been called and chosen: work all the harder to justify it. (2 Pt. 1:10)

If Yahweh set his heart on you and chose you, it was not because you outnumbered other peoples . . . It was for love of you. (Dt. 7:7–8)

Be consecrated to me, because I, Yahweh, am holy, and I will set you apart from all these peoples so that you may be mine. (Lv. 20:26)

You are a chosen race, a royal priesthood, a consecrated nation, a people set apart to sing the praises of God who called you out of the darkness into his wonderful light. (1 Pt. 2:9)

Before I formed you in the womb I knew you;
before you came to birth I consecrated you;
I have appointed you as prophet to the nations. (Jr. 1:5)

———∞———

## For Further Reflection

Happy the man you choose, whom you invite
to live in your courts. (Ps. 65:4)

To the holy people of Jesus Christ, who are called to take their place among all the saints everywhere who pray to our Lord Jesus Christ. (1 Co. 1:2)

Mary, do not be afraid; you have won God's favor. *(See* Lk. 1:26–38)

# 5

# FATHERHOOD OF GOD

It is the Lord's Prayer which expresses most completely the Fatherhood of God. Here we have the prayer Jesus used to confirm his own relationship with the Father, the prayer he willingly shared with his disciples and with us so that we too might acknowledge that God is our Father.

In a world sensitive to male/female definitions and appropriations, however, it might seem unusual that we would continue to call God, "Father." After all, could it not just as well be "Mother" or "Friend" or . . . ? To be tied into such a speculation seems a waste of time. Try to remember, however, that Father is not meant to communicate a sexual identity as much as a possible "gender" identity. This does not imply, of course, that one gender is better than the other, but that Father as gender says something to us about God as he relates to the Son.

Far better for us to allow the Spirit to teach us the meaning of Father as Jesus recognized it, rather than be limited to the notion of Father as we experience it within a cultural context. For further thought on the notion of gender, read C. S. Lewis's Space Trilogy.

## Scripture Verses

And I was thinking:
How I wanted to rank you with my sons,
and give you a country of delights,
the fairest heritage of all the nations!

I had thought you would call me: My father,
and would never cease to follow me. (Jr. 3:19)


O foolish, unwise people!
Is not this your father, who gave you being,
who made you, by whom you subsist?
Think back on the days of old,
think over the years, down the ages.
Ask of your father, let him teach you.
(Dt. 32:6–7)


The Fatherhood of God. (Lk. 15:11–32)


In your prayers do not babble as the pagans do, for they
think that by using many words they will make themselves
heard. Do not be like them; your Father knows what you need
before you ask him. (Mt. 6:7–9)


Our Father in heaven,
may your name be held holy,
your kingdom come,
your will be done,
on earth as in heaven.
Give us today our daily bread.
And forgive us our debts,
as we have forgiven those who are in debt to us.
And do not put us to the test,
but save us from the evil one.
(Mt. 6:9–13)

The proof that you are sons is that God has sent the Spirit of his Son into our hearts: the Spirit that cries, "Abba, Father," and it is this that makes you a son. (Ga. 4:6–7)

Blessed be God the Father of our Lord Jesus Christ, who has blessed us with all the spiritual blessings of heaven in Christ. Before the world was made, he chose us, chose us in Christ, . . . determining that we should become his adopted sons, through Jesus Christ. (Ep. 1:1–14)

---

## For Further Reflection

Let me proclaim Yahweh's decree;
he has told me, "You are my son,
today I have become your father.
Ask and I will give you the nations for your heritage,
the ends of the earth for your domain . . ."
(Ps. 2:7–8)

I will keep my love for him always,
my covenant with him shall stand.
(Ps. 89:28)

"He will invoke me, 'My father,
my God and rock of my safety,'
and I shall make him my first-born,
the Most High for kings on earth." (Ps. 89:26–27)

# 6

# PRAISE THE LORD!

When praying these scripture passages, try to allow your body to speak and to listen. All too often we constrict God's Word within us by constricting our bodies with sedentary, immobile positions which are "physically" closed in appearance and in actuality. We have a great deal to learn in this area from men and women involved in the charismatic renewal movement within the churches. They have learned how to praise the Lord in song, in gesture, and in speech.

Try during your meditation period to use song. Close the door, put on a record, and sing along. St. Augustine says that singing is praying twice! Sometime during the day use gestures: extend your hands in prayer, or fold them in praise-filled reverence. The people of the Old Testament danced, sang, shouted, and jubilated in the reality of their God. We are invited to do the same.

Finally, in speech. Don't be afraid; no one is recording your words. Use words of praise over and over again: "Glory to you, Lord," "Praise you, Lord Jesus," "Alleluia." Let them become a normal part of your vocabulary, and you will begin to understand and to feel within the depth of your being what it means to "Bless the God of gods."

## Scripture Verses

I will bless Yahweh at all times,
his praise shall be on my lips continually;

my soul glories in Yahweh,
let the humble hear and rejoice.
Proclaim with me the greatness of Yahweh,
together let us extol his name. (Ps. 34:1–3)


They shouted aloud, "Victory to our God, who sits on the
throne, and to the Lamb!" . . . And all . . . prostrated themselves before the throne . . . worshiping God with these
words, "Amen. Praise and glory and wisdom and thanksgiving
and honor and power and strength to our God for ever and
ever. Amen." (Rv. 7:10–12)


May you be blessed, Yahweh, the God of Israel our ancestor,
for ever and for ever! Yours, Yahweh, is the greatness, the
power, splendor . . . sovereignty . . . You are exalted over
all . . . At this time, our God, we give you glory, we praise the
splendor of your name. (1 Ch. 29:10–13)


May you be blessed, Lord, God of our ancestors,
be praised and extolled for ever.
Blessed be your glorious and holy name,
praised and extolled for ever.
. . . All you who worship him, bless the God of gods,
praise him and give him thanks,
for his love is everlasting. (Dn. 3:52–90)


Invitation to praise God. (Si. 39:13–21)


Mary's Magnificat. (Lk. 1:46–55)

Benedictus. (Lk. 1:68–79)

———————&———————

## For Further Reflection

Come, let us praise Yahweh joyfully,
acclaiming the Rock of our safety. *(See* Ps. 95:1–6)

*Cosmic Hymn of Praise*
Let heaven praise Yahweh. (Ps. 148)

Let everything that breathes praise Yahweh! (Ps. 150)

# 7

# GOD'S PROMISE TO HIS PEOPLE

God's promise, in reality, is a promise to be faithful to himself. He who is love had chosen humankind to be his image. We, however, chose to break the image within through our sinfulness. God remained faithful to his promise, however. He who chose us would not abandon us to our sinfulness, but would continue to "choose" us again and again.

And so the Son is sent into our flesh so that the promise can materialize, so that the promise can be fulfilled. Now, again in our frail frame, God perfectly echoes through the person of Jesus Christ the Lord. Now, in the flesh of a human being, the image of God is restored, and accepted, thereby integrating the infinite with the finite, the transitory with the eternal. This takes place in Jesus, born of Mary.

God's promise, therefore, is a promise to continue to love. It is a promise that shows love to the point of death. It is a promise to be for ever with us. It is a promise to be us, no, to let us be him in some mysterious way.

## Scripture Verses

"My Lord Yahweh," Abram replied, "what do you intend to give me? I go childless . . ." And then this word of Yahweh was spoken to him, . . . "Look up to heaven and count the stars if you can. Such will be your descendants," he told him. Abram put his faith in Yahweh. (Gn. 15:2–6)

All that the Father gives me will come to me,
and whoever comes to me
I shall not turn him away. (Jn. 6:37)


If your lips confess that Jesus is Lord and if you believe in your
heart that God raised him from the dead, then you will be
saved. (Rm. 10:9)


Yes, God loved the world so much
that he gave his only Son,
so that everyone who believes in him may not be lost
but may have eternal life. (Jn. 3:16)


He will make his home among them . . . his name is God-
with-them. He will wipe away all tears from their eyes; there
will be no more death, and no more mourning or sadness.
(Rv. 21:3–4)


I will give water from the well of life free to anybody who is
thirsty . . . I will be his God and he a son to me. (Rv. 21:6–7)


Then Peter spoke. "What about us?" he said to him. "We
have left everything and followed you. What are we to have,
then?" Jesus said to him, ". . . when all is made new . . . you
will yourselves sit on twelve thrones to judge the twelve tribes
of Israel. And everyone who has left houses, brothers, . . . for

the sake of my name will be repaid a hundred times over, and also inherit eternal life." (Mt. 19:27–29)

———————⟨∞⟩———————

## *For Further Reflection*

God has given us eternal life
and this life is in his Son;
anyone who has the Son has life. (1 Jn. 5:11–12)

If you obey my voice and hold fast to my covenant, you of all the nations shall be my very own, for all the earth is mine. (Ex. 19:5)

I am the bread of life.
He who comes to me will never be hungry;
he who believes in me will never thirst. (Jn. 6:35)

# 8

# GOD'S FAITHFULNESS AND FIDELITY

The faithfulness and fidelity of God go beyond our wildest imaginings. That one would remain loyal to that which was not loyal in return goes against common sense. Yet that is God, Yahweh, the faithful one.

Here is an opportunity for us to review our own faithfulness and fidelity to God: our faithfulness in prayer, in speech, in action. Do the things we do and say convey what we really want conveyed about our belief and acceptance of the Lord? God himself showed us the power of faithfulness when he sent his Son into the world to die for our sins. He showed the power and depth of true fidelity when he shared with us his very life in the sending of the Spirit. He shows us the constancy of his Word to us when he remembers the covenant made so long ago with Abraham, and made present now in Jesus.

Take heart, therefore, that One is faithful, and that he calls us to be faithful in return. Start with yourself, where God dwells within. Be faithful to the image he has placed within you. Then be faithful in love to your family, friends, and neighbors. The image of God is there also. Finally, to those whom we find difficult to accept. God is there also. Be faithful as he is.

## Scripture Verses

We may be unfaithful, but he is always faithful, for he cannot disown his own self. (2 Tm. 2:13)

[God] will keep you steady and without blame . . . because God by calling you has joined you to his Son, Jesus Christ; and God is faithful. (1 Co. 1:8–9)

I, I am Yahweh,
there is no other savior but me.
It is I who have spoken, have saved, . . .
not any strangers among you . . .
I am your God, I am he from eternity. (Is. 43:11–13)

Yahweh passed before him [Moses] and proclaimed, "Yahweh, Yahweh, a God of tenderness and compassion, slow to anger, rich in kindness and faithfulness." (Ex. 34:6)

In the same way, when God wanted to make the heirs to the promise thoroughly realize that his purpose was unalterable, he conveyed this by an oath; . . . Here we have an anchor for our soul, as sure as it is firm. (Heb. 6:17–19)

God has called you and he will not fail you. (1 Th. 5:24)

Jesus's death is a witness to God's faithfulness. (Heb. 12:1–4)

---

## For Further Reflection

I will not break my covenant,
I will not revoke my given word;
I have sworn on my holiness, once for all,
and cannot turn liar to David. (Ps. 89:34–35)


The Sons of Israel . . . cried out for help and from the depths
of their slavery their cry came up to God. God heard their
groaning and he called to mind his covenant with Abraham,
Isaac, and Jacob. (Ex. 2:23–24)


God will always be true even though everyone proves to be
false; . . . our lack of holiness makes God demonstrate his integrity. (Rm. 3:4)

# 9

# OFFER A PLEASING SACRIFICE TO GOD

It's easy to get caught up in our cultural propensity to "do things." If I do "such and such," then I am assured a particular result will take place: if I study, I am more assured that I will pass; if I practice, then I am more assured that I will win; if I give, I am more assured that I will receive. Tit for tat is not an uncommon mind-set in our Western culture.

God, however, is not looking for that. He is not looking for a tit-for-tat relationship. He's looking for a pure heart, a cleansed heart, a true heart. Fasts, strict penances, acts of mortification, etc., will be useless, unless a pure heart emerges. God cannot be bribed: Saying *x* number of rosaries, fasting from certain foods, helping everyone on the block will not please the Lord unless our hearts are broken and purified. This is the sacrifice he desires; this is the sacrifice he accepts.

From the scripture passages chosen, you can easily see how this is made practical in our relationships with one another. How we relate to the Body of Christ, God's people, gives us an indication as to how we are relating to God. Are we approaching one another in humility? Are we striving to assist one another with no questions asked? Are we offering ourselves to one another as Jesus offers himself to humankind? This is the sacrifice pleasing to the Lord.

There is no need, however, to become overly scrupulous or discouraged. Surely we are not able to offer the "perfect" sacrifice—only the Lord Jesus has been able to do this. But we can offer ourselves, today, as best as we are able. Begin in your prayer to seek God's direction for your life. Ask him to use the scripture passages available under this theme to show you where you are offering a sacrifice that is pleasing, and where you have yet to move in that direction. Trust he will tell you.

## Scripture Verses

I take no pleasure in your solemn festivals . . .
Let me have no more of the din of your chanting . . .
But let justice flow like water,
and integrity like an unfailing stream. (Am. 5:21–24)

What are your endless sacrifices to me?
says Yahweh . . .
Bring me your worthless offerings no more, . . .
I shall not listen . . .
Take your wrong-doing out of my sight.
Cease to do evil.
Learn to do good,
search for justice,
help the oppressed
be just to the orphan,
plead for the widow. (Is. 1:11–17)

With what gift shall I come into Yahweh's presence
and bow down before God on high? . . .
This is what Yahweh asks of you:
only this, to act justly,

to love tenderly
and to walk humbly with your God. (Mi. 6:6–8)

Christ's perfect sacrifice offered for us was one of obedience
through suffering. (Heb. 5:1–10)

To love [God] with all your heart . . . and to love your neighbor as yourself, this is far more important than any holocaust or
sacrifice. (Mk. 12:33)

Keep doing good works and sharing your resources, for these
are sacrifices that please God. (Heb. 13:16)

[Samuel replied]
Is the pleasure of Yahweh in holocausts and sacrifices
or in obedience to the voice of Yahweh?
Yes, obedience is better than sacrifice,
submissiveness better than the fat of rams. (1 Sm. 15:22)

---

## *For Further Reflection*

Lord, now we are the least of all nations, . . .
But may the contrite soul, the humbled spirit be as acceptable
    to you . . .
as thousands of fattened lambs: . . .
and may it be your will that we follow you wholeheartedly.
(Dn. 3:37–40)

Let thanksgiving be your sacrifice to God,
fulfill the vows you make to the Most High. (Ps. 50:14)


Paul exhorts us to offer our bodies as a "holy sacrifice" by
changing our behavior. (Rm. 12:1–2)

# 10

# ADOPTED AS HIS OWN

Perhaps you are blessed with an adopted child. My good friends are, and I am honored to be the godparent. Their relationship with the child has blessed me with an insight as to the way God loves us, his children. From the very beginning I noticed that they always introduced Robert as their son. Never their adopted son; simply their son. They made no distinction between their adopted child, and a child that was not adopted. All were the same.

So it is with us. God has adopted us as his sons/daughters. We have been chosen as his own, not through our own right, but because of his generous love—in the same way that my godson had been chosen because of the generous love of his parents. And so God treats us exactly as he treats his Son, Jesus: he loves us in the same way; protects us and cares for us in the same way; disciplines us in the same way, etc. There is, in his eyes, no difference.

I find this hard to imagine, yet that is how God loves us. Think about it: we are, in a sense, no different from Jesus in God's eyes and heart. He gives us both the same Spirit, the same love, the same attention. The only difference is that Jesus had responded from before time began, whereas I keep pushing my sonship aside. Do you?

Spend time with this theme, thanking the Lord for calling you a son/daughter. Spend time delighting in the reality of his love. It is that same love which raised Jesus from the dead and it will raise us also from the deadness of our lives, the deadness of our sins, the deadness of our flesh.

## Scripture Verses

Everyone moved by the Spirit is a son of God. The spirit you received is not the spirit of slaves bringing fear into your lives again; it is the spirit of sons, and it makes us cry out, "Abba, Father!" (Rm. 8:14–15)

You are sons of Yahweh your God . . . Yahweh has chosen you to be his very own people out of all the peoples of the earth. (Dt. 14:1–2)

When the appointed time came, God sent his Son . . . to enable us to be adopted as sons. The proof that you are sons is that God has sent the Spirit of his Son into our hearts . . . it is this that makes you a son. (Ga. 4:4–7)

Before the world was made, he chose us, he chose us in Christ, to be holy and spotless, and to live through love in his presence, determining that we should become his adopted sons, through Jesus Christ.
. . . . in whom, through his blood, we gain our freedom, the forgiveness of our sins. (Ep. 1:4–7)

Think of the love that the father has lavished on us,
by letting us be called God's children;
and that is what we are. (1 Jn. 3:1)

But to all who did accept him
he gave power to become children of God. (Jn. 1:12)

In his great mercy he has given us a new birth as his sons, by
raising Jesus Christ from the dead, so that we have a sure hope
and the promise of an inheritance . . . [that is] being kept for
you in the heavens. (1 Pt. 1:3–4)

## *For Further Reflection*

He will invoke me, "My father,
my God and rock of my safety,"
and I shall make him my first-born . . .
I will keep my love for him always. (Ps. 89:26–28)

How I wanted to rank you with my sons . . .
I had thought you would call me: My father,
and would never cease to follow me. (Jr. 3:19)

Father of orphans . . .
such is God in his holy dwelling. (Ps. 68:5)

# 11

# LOVE OF NEIGHBOR

When praying these passages, spend some time with the Good Samaritan. Instead of looking at it in the obvious way, however, I suggest that you be the innkeeper in the story. More than likely you have been the "innkeeper" before; i.e., you've been the person left holding the bag. In many ways it was probably easy for the Good Samaritan to pick up the wounded person, nurse him, and take him to the inn. It was the innkeeper, however, who had to continue the process. He was left with the full-time job of nursing the individual back to health.

I think that Jesus, as the Good Samaritan, does this to us. He picks us up, binds up our wounds, but then he entrusts us into the hands of someone else, fully expecting that the individual will continue the process.

Love of neighbor, therefore, goes beyond the immediate; it goes beyond one-time care. Jesus fully expects us to be the innkeeper who continues the process he has begun. He has given us the privilege of nursing back to health, through our love and presence, those who have been given to us. Remember always that each person whom Jesus, the Good Samaritan, sends to us is a gift from him to us.

As we ask the Spirit to show us "Who is our neighbor," let us also ask him to open our hearts to receive the neighbor that the Lord sends into our midst.

## Scripture Verses

Let us love one another
since love comes from God
and everyone who loves is begotten by God and knows God.
Anyone who fails to love can never have known God,
because God is love. (1 Jn. 4:7–8)


I give you a new commandment:
love one another;
just as I have loved you,
you must also love one another.
By this love you have for one another,
everyone will know that you are my disciples. (Jn. 13:34–35)


Jesus said, "You must love the Lord your God with all your
heart, with all your soul, and with all your mind . . . You
must love your neighbor as yourself." (Mt. 22:37–39)


*The Good Samaritan*
"Who is my neighbor?" (Lk. 10:29–37)


"Lord, when did we see you hungry and feed you; or thirsty
and give you drink? . . . a stranger and make you welcome;
naked and clothe you; sick or in prison and go to see you?" And
the King will answer, ". . . in so far as you did this to one of

the least of these brothers of mine, you did it to me."
(Mt. 25:37–40; *see* 31–46)

Anybody not living a holy life
and not loving his brother
is no child of God's . . .
If you refuse to love, you must remain dead. (1 Jn. 3:10–15)

Serve one another . . . in works of love, since the whole of the
Law is summarized in a single command: Love your neighbor
as yourself. (Ga. 5:13–14)

---

## For Further Reflection

Avoid getting into debt, except the debt of mutual love. If
you love your fellow men you have carried out your obligations
. . . Love is the one thing that cannot hurt your neighbor; that
is why it is the answer to every one of the commandments.
(Rm. 13:8–10)

Anyone who loves his brother is living in the light. (1 Jn. 2:10)

This is my commandment:
love one another,
as I have loved you.
A man can have no greater love
than to lay down his life for his friends. (Jn. 15:12–14)

# 12

# REJECTION BY FRIEND OR FOE

Often our faithfulness to the Lord will bring about rejection. It's a difficult thing to bear, especially if your heart is bound to the one who has rejected you. Yet Jesus himself warns us that this might happen (Lk. 6:22–23).

Notice, however, why the rejection takes place—"on account of the Son of Man." It would be incorrect to assume that every time we are rejected by someone that we are being rejected because of our relationship to the Lord. If only this were the case. Sometimes—we have to be honest—we are rejected because some part of our personality deserves rejection: a sharp tongue, a judgmental spirit, a haughty disposition.

Before we claim martyrdom, therefore, make sure that the rejection is "on account of the Son of Man"; make sure that the rejection stems from our rootedness in Jesus rather than our rootedness in a self-centered attitude that needs changing.

To be rejected for the name of Jesus is a blessing; to claim that we are being rejected for his name, however, when it is really our pride and stubbornness that is being criticized, is a lie.

## Scripture Verses

[Jesus] said to them, ". . . the Son of Man is about to be handed over to the chief priests and scribes. They will condemn him to death and will hand him over to the pagans to be

mocked and scourged and crucified; and on the third day he
will rise again." (Mt. 20:17–19)

Peter was sitting outside in the courtyard, and a servant girl
came up to him and said, "You too were with Jesus the Gali-
lean." But he denied it in front of them all . . . then he started
calling down curses on himself and swearing, "I do not know
the man." At that moment the cock crew. (Mt. 26:69–75)

[Jesus] was still speaking when a number of men appeared,
and at the head of them a man called Judas, one of the Twelve,
who went up to Jesus to kiss him. Jesus said, "Judas, are you
betraying the Son of Man with a kiss?" (Lk. 22:47–48)

Anyone who rejects you rejects me, and those who reject me
reject the one who sent me. (Lk. 10:16)

He was in the world
that had its beginning through him,
and the world did not know him.
He came to his own domain
and his own people did not accept him. (Jn. 1:10–11)

My friends and my companions shrink from my wounds,
even the dearest of them keep their distance; . . .
Yahweh, do not desert me,
do not stand aside, my God! (Ps. 38:11–21)

Happy are you when people hate you, drive you out, abuse you, denounce your name as criminal, on account of the Son of Man. Rejoice when that day comes and dance for joy, for then your reward will be great in heaven. (Lk. 6:22–23)

---

## *For Further Reflection*

I tell you solemnly, no prophet is ever accepted in his own country. (Lk. 4:24)

To everyone of my oppressors
I am contemptible,
loathsome to my neighbors,
to my friends a thing of fear.
Those who see me in the street
hurry past me; . . .
But I put my trust in you, Yahweh,
I say, "You are my God." (Ps. 31:11–14)

All those who used to be my friends
watched for my downfall, . . .
But Yahweh is at my side, a mighty hero. *(See* Jr. 20:7–13)

# 13

## COME BACK TO ME

Why do we have to "come back" to the Lord, if he never leaves us? If his love is as infinite as we claim, why do we have to return to him? Returning implies that somehow we were separated. Yet is that not contrary to our belief that he is always present?

To "come back" to the Lord is not a contradiction, but the statement of a reality. The fact that God is always present to us does not change; he remains constant: dwelling within, never leaving us. Coming back to God, therefore, is meant to touch us on a different level. It urges us to give every part of our being to him; to allow his Spirit access to every thought, word, and deed. Each one of these areas is meant to be a channel through which the Lord gifts us. However, we often refuse the gift of his love, so we need to "come back." We need to "come back" to the reality that he is the Giver of all, that we are to receive gratefully and thankfully all that he offers.

The "evil" and the "iniquity" that shroud our vision, according to the psalmist, are really those times we do not acknowledge his power, presence, and generosity. They are the times we think ourselves as the source, rather than proclaim him as the Source. And so the Spirit within us cries out, "Come back to your God" so we can come back to the reality of life itself.

## Scripture Verses

Come back to me with all your heart, . . .
Let your hearts be broken, not your garments torn,
turn to Yahweh your God again,
for he is all tenderness and compassion. (Jl. 2:12–13)

Little by little, therefore, you correct those who offend,
you admonish and remind them of how they have sinned,
so that they may abstain from evil and trust in you, Lord.
(Ws. 12:2)

Israel, come back to your God;
your iniquity was the cause of your downfall.
. . . come back to Yahweh.
Say to him, "Take all iniquity away . . ." (Ho. 14:2–3)

Think where you were before you fell; repent, and do as you
used to at first. (Rv. 2:5)

Israel, I will not forget you.
I have dispelled your faults like a cloud,
your sins like a mist.
Come back to me, for I have redeemed you. (Is. 44:21–22)

I am the one who reproves and disciplines all those he loves: so repent in real earnest. Look, I am standing at the door, knocking. If one of you hears me calling and opens the door, I will come in to share his meal, side by side with him. (Rv. 3:19–20)

"The time has come," he [Jesus] said, "and the kingdom of God is close at hand. Repent, and believe the Good News." (Mk. 1:15)

———❧———

## For Further Reflection

Turn again, then, to your God,
hold fast to love and justice,
and always put your trust in your God. (Ho. 12:7)

You are merciful to all, because you can do all things
and overlook men's sins so that they can repent. (Ws. 11:23)

God overlooked that sort of thing when men were ignorant, but now he is telling everyone everywhere that they must repent. (Ac. 17:30)

# 14

# CHRIST RECONCILES US

The process of reconciliation is very much like knitting. Made in the image of God, we have torn ourselves away from the main part of the fabric; we remain loose ends, no longer woven and connected to the whole. And so we need to be knitted back into the design, into the pattern, into the whole.

This cannot be accomplished alone. Only one who knows and accepts completely the entire design can do it. This is Jesus. He knows and accepts the design of love that his Father has woven for us. Unlike us, Jesus does not desire to employ another design, another pattern, to express the infinite love of God. The pattern of love offered, of love received, of love shared is his pattern because it is the pattern of his Father in heaven.

And so, in his flesh, Jesus reconciles us by accepting and implementing once again the pattern of love which is the very essence of the Father. This pattern requires giving with no guarantee of return; it requires dying to self; it requires death. Jesus alone said "Yes" to this in every part of his being. He alone said "Yes" to all that it implied. In him, therefore, we are reconciled, because now, in him, we too can say "Yes" to the Father's pattern of love.

## Scripture Verses

When **we** were reconciled to God by the death of his Son, we were still enemies; now that we have been reconciled, surely we may count on being saved by the life of his Son. (Rm. 5:10)

In other words, God in Christ was reconciling the world to himself, not holding men's faults against them, and he has entrusted to us the news that they are reconciled.
*(See* 2 Co. 5:18–21)

God wanted all perfection
to be found in him
and all things to be reconciled through him and for him,
everything in heaven and everything on earth,
when he made peace
by his death on the cross. (Col. 1:19–20)

Not long ago you were foreigners and enemies . . . but now he has reconciled you, . . . in that mortal body. (Col. 1:21–22)

When the kindness and love of God our savior for mankind were revealed, it was not because he was concerned with any righteous actions we might have done ourselves; . . . he saved us by means of the cleansing water of rebirth and by renewing us with the Holy Spirit which he so generously poured over us through Jesus Christ our Savior. (Tt. 3:4–6)

Christ suffered for you . . . he was insulted . . . tortured . . . bearing our faults in his own body on the cross, so that we might die to our own faults and live for holiness; through his wounds you have been healed. (1 Pt. 2:21–24)

And yet ours were the sufferings he bore,
ours the sorrows he carried.

. . . he was pierced through for our faults,
crushed for our sins.
On him lies a punishment that brings us peace
and through his wounds we are healed. (Is. 53:4–5)

---

## *For Further Reflection*

For he is the peace between us . . . and by restoring peace
through the cross . . . both of us have in the one Spirit our
way to come to the Father. (Ep. 2:14–18)

Both Jew and pagan sinned . . . and both are justified through
the free gift of his grace by being redeemed in Christ Jesus who
was appointed by God to sacrifice his life so as to win reconciliation through faith. (Rm. 3:23–25)

We had all gone astray like sheep,
each taking his own way.
And Yahweh burdened him
with the sins of all of us.
Harshly dealt with, he bore it humbly. (Is. 53:6–7)

# 15

# COMMUNITY/FELLOWSHIP

It is within community that we are given the opportunity to grow in the Lord. This occurs because within community we are most specifically given the opportunity to die to self. It is not an easy thing to do, this dying; it is not an easy thing to give and not expect a return. If, however, we intend to grow into the fullness of Christ, we will need to grow fully in all that Christ is: love freely given with no price asked. This is why Jesus is the cornerstone (Ep. 2:20–22); this is why we are expected to lean on him, find our support on him, rest on him.

In today's Church, more and more people are realizing that community is necessary for their growth in the Lord. They are making choices which enable them to die to self so they might rise in Christ. The choices are difficult, often involving work, school, money, recreation, friends. Perhaps you are struggling with similar choices. If so, keep in mind that true union with the Father, Son, and Spirit will necessarily involve union with humankind in whom Father, Son, and Spirit dwell.

## Scripture Verses

Now you together are Christ's body; but each of you is a different part of it. *(See* 1 Co. 12:27–30)

What we have seen and heard
we are telling you

so that you too may be in union with us,
as we are in union
with the Father
and with his son Jesus Christ. (1 Jn. 1:3)


Be united; . . . and the God of love and peace will be with
you. Greet one another with the holy kiss. (2 Co. 13:11–12)


Do not forget: thin sowing means thin reaping; the more you
sow, the more you reap. Each one should give what he has
decided in his own mind, not grudgingly, or because he is made
to, for God loves a cheerful giver. (2 Co. 9:6–7)


Just as a human body, though it is made up of many parts, is
a single unit because all these parts, though many, made one
body, so it is with Christ. In the one Spirit we were all baptized,
Jew as well as Greeks, slaves as well as citizens.
(1 Co. 12:12–13)


You are part of a building that has the apostles and prophets for
its foundations, and Christ Jesus himself for its main cornerstone . . . And you too, in him, are being built into a house
where God lives, in the Spirit. (Ep. 2:20–22)


The saints together make a unity in the work of service, building up the body of Christ. In this way we are all to come to
unity in our faith and in our knowledge of the Son of God, until
we become the perfect Man, fully mature with the fullness of
Christ himself. (Ep. 4:12–13)

---

## *For Further Reflection*

The faithful all lived together and owned everything in common . . .

They went as a body to the Temple every day but met in their houses for the breaking of bread; . . . they praised God and were looked up to by everyone. (Ac. 2:44–47)

How good, how delightful it is
for all to live together like brothers. (*See* Ps. 133)

Let us be concerned for each other, to stir a response in love and good works. Do not stay away from the meetings of the community, as some do, but encourage each other to go. (Heb. 10:24–25)

# 16

# POWER OF GOD'S WORD

Alive and active. This describes the power of God's Word as succinctly as possible. It is a Word which brings forth what it intends: a Word which creates, saves, redeems, and heals. It is God present to his people in a way that allows us to "hear" him whom we cannot see.

This Word is meant to be food for us—food for our journey to the Father. In a sense, it is another source of the heavenly bread which Jesus refers to in the eucharistic passages of St. John. This Word of God can nourish and guide us, providing us with the "sense of direction" needed as we journey through the dark forest within.

Today's world has tried to compromise God's Word, by bombarding us with useless words from every direction: mindless lyrics, infantile commercials, deceptive slogans, etc. As a people who cherish and treasure the true Word, let us hold it with reverence in our heart, savoring its every nuance, seeking its guidance and power in every situation of our lives. The world will not accept such a stance, yet it is precisely this stance which is rooted in the Lord.

In preparation for praying these passages, therefore, ask the Lord to clear your heart of useless words. Ask him to purify you from the confusing use of such standard words as "love," "commitment," "friend," "spouse," etc. In doing so we will be open to hearing the true Word echo within through the passages chosen for prayer.

## Scripture Verses

The words I have spoken to you are spirit
and they are life. (Jn. 6:63)


Man does not live on bread alone
but on every word that comes from the mouth of God. (Mt. 4:4)


The word of God is something alive and active: it cuts like
any double-edged sword but more finely: It can slip through the
place where the soul is divided from the spirit, or joints from
the marrow; it can judge the secret emotions and thoughts.
(Heb. 4:12)


The Law of Yahweh is perfect.
new life for the soul;
The decree of Yahweh is trustworthy,
wisdom for the simple.
The precepts of Yahweh are upright,
joy for the heart;
The commandment of Yahweh is clear,
light for the eyes. (Ps. 19:7–8)


In the beginning was the Word:
the Word was with God
and the Word was God.

He was with God in the beginning.
Through him all things came to be,
not one thing had its being but through him. (Jn. 1:1–3)

Yes, as the rain and the snow come down from the heavens and
do not return without watering the earth, . . . so the word
that goes from my mouth does not return to me empty, without
carrying out my will and succeeding in what it was sent to do.
(Is. 55:10–11)

God's spoken Word was creative. (Gn. 1:1–2; 4)

———————⟨∞⟩———————

## *For Further Reflection*

The Word of God is the sword of the Spirit. (Ep. 6:17)

Down from the heavens, from the royal throne, leaped your
    all-powerful Word; . . .
Carrying your unambiguous command like a sharp sword.
(Ws. 18:15)

By my own self I swear it;
what comes from my mouth is truth,
a word irrevocable. (Is. 45:23)

# 17

# IN TIMES OF PERSECUTION

The companion word to persecution is powerlessness. To accept true persecution in the name of Jesus demands that we respond with powerlessness, placing our trust in the Lord.

Jesus is the example here. Confronted with persecution due to his teaching, life-style, and challenging word, he embraced powerlessness as the key to victory. This response confounded the sensibilities of the world that had accepted power as the only acceptable response to persecution: power which tried to overthrow, power which fought back, power which defended, power which tried to meet the enemy on its own terms.

Such was not the course of action Jesus took. He refused to meet the Enemy on any terms but the terms of love which the Father had placed deep within. He refused to confront the Enemy eye to eye except through the eyes and the embrace of love. This is what brought him victory.

A lesson, therefore, is learned. Should we be persecuted for bearing his Name, we are called to respond with powerlessness. We have no need to defend anything except the reality of Christ crucified raised from the dead. By remaining faithful to that reality, we will indeed remain faithful to all that is good and true and just. It was so for him, and will be for us.

This does not mean, of course, that we are called to be inactive and passive. Quite the contrary. In times of persecution we are to be active and aggressive: active in loving, and aggressive in giving. But this comes about in accepting powerlessness as he did.

## Scripture Verses

Happy those who are persecuted in the cause of right: theirs is the kingdom of heaven.
Happy are you when people abuse you and persecute you and speak all kinds of calumny against you on my account. Rejoice and be glad, for your reward will be great in heaven. (Mt. 5:10–12)

As scripture promised: For your sake we are being massacred daily, and reckoned as sheep for the slaughter. These are the trials through which we triumph, by the power of him who loved us. (Rm. 8:36–37)

You know, though, what I have taught, . . . all the persecutions I have endured; and the Lord has rescued me from every one of them. You are well aware, then, that anybody who tries to live in devotion to Christ is certain to be attacked. (2 Tm. 3:10–12)

Take pity on me, God, as they harry me,
pressing their attacks home all day.
All day my opponents harry me,
hordes coming in to attack.
Raise me up when I am most afraid
I put my trust in you. (*See* Ps. 56)

Remember the words I said to you:
A servant is not greater than his master.
If they persecuted me,
they will persecute you too. (Jn. 15:20)

Bless those who persecute you: never curse them, bless them. (Rm. 12:14)

Men will seize you and persecute you; they will hand you over . . . because of my name—and that will be your opportunity to bear witness . . . I myself shall give you an eloquence and a wisdom that none of your opponents will be able to resist . . . not a hair of your head will be lost. Your endurance will win you your life. (Lk. 21:12–19)

———∞———

## *For Further Reflection*

Blessed be the God and Father of our Lord Jesus Christ, a gentle Father and the God of all consolation, who comforts us in all our sorrows, so that we can offer others, in their sorrows, the consolation that we have received from God ourselves. (2 Co. 1:3–4)

And they had the apostles called in, gave orders for them to be flogged, warned them not to speak in the name of Jesus and released them. And so they left the presence of the Sanhedrin

glad to have had the honor of suffering humiliation for the sake
of the name. (Ac. 5:40–41)


I call on God the Most High . . .
to check the people harrying me,
may God send his faithfulness and love. (*See* Ps. 57)

# 18

# OUR PRAYERS ARE ANSWERED

All of us have had prayers answered, and all of us have had prayers which were not answered. At least, not answered in the ways we wanted. Yet scripture says clearly, ask in the name of Jesus and it will be granted. Our practical experience however, is that this does not always seem to "work." Unless we understand the "why," we might lose heart and eventually faith.

There are several ways of approaching this question. First, we need to admit that God might say no. Trusting in his love will allow us to hear the no without rancor and dismay. Also, the Lord may be trying to give us a gift which we have not been willing to receive. For example, if our heart is set on a particular favor, and another is offered, we may not be able to appreciate that which has been given because we remain fixed on the favor for which we yearn. The same is true with the Lord. He often answers our prayers in a way that is far better, but we do not accept the gift offered because we had our heart set on one thing rather than on receiving all that he offers.

Finally, our prayers may not be answered because we do not really ask in his name. When we ask in his name, we ask for what we need. Usually, however, the very last thing to which we are willing to die, is the belief that God will grant us any wish, rather than provide for every need.

## Scripture Verses

But when you pray, go to your private room and, when you have shut the door, pray to your Father who is in that secret place, and your Father who sees all that is done in secret will reward you. (Mt. 6:6)

Ask and it will be given to you; search and you will find; knock, and the door will be opened to you. *(See* Mt. 7:7–10)

I tell you solemnly once again, if two of you on earth agree to ask anything at all, it will be granted to you by my Father in heaven. For when two or three meet in my name, I shall be there with them. (Mt. 18:19–20)

Whatever you ask for in my name I will do,
so that the Father may be glorified in the Son.
If you ask for anything in my name,
I will do it. (Jn. 14:13–14)

We are quite confident that if we ask for anything,
and it is in accordance with his will,
he will hear us;
and, knowing that whatever we may ask, he hears us,
we know that we have already been granted what we ask of
    him. (1 Jn. 5:14–15)

Yahweh . . . says this, Call to me and I will answer you; I will tell you great mysteries of which you know nothing. (Jr. 33:2)

The Spirit too comes to help us in our weakness. For when we cannot choose words in order to pray properly, the Spirit himself expresses our plea in a way that could never be put into words, and God . . . knows perfectly well what he means. (Rm. 8:26–27)

---

## For Further Reflection

If you remain in me
and my words remain in you,
you may ask what you will
and you shall get it. (Jn. 15:7)

And if you have faith, everything you ask for in prayer you will receive. (Mt. 21:22)

If there is anything you need, pray for it, asking God for it with prayer and thanksgiving. (Ph. 4:6)

# 19

# GOD DWELLS WITHIN

Being temples of the Holy Spirit gives us a special responsibility to care for ourselves in the same way we would care for any sacred place or object. It is not incorrect to say that we are, in a sense, tabernacles of the Lord, and are meant to treat one another, and ourselves, with respect and reverence, just as we would treat the Blessed Sacrament present in the tabernacle.

A balance, therefore, is needed if we are to hear the voice of the Lord echoing within. Regular exercise, diet, recreation, and rest will enable us to hear the Lord more clearly, and respond more wholeheartedly to his promptings.

In addition, within the balanced routine that leads to a healthy body, we will be able to pray. While working, resting, exercising, etc. we will be sensitized to the Lord's Spirit so that each one of those activities becomes a joy for us. Try and you will see.

## Scripture Verses

Didn't you realize you were God's temple and that the Spirit of God was living among you? (1 Co. 3:16)

Your body, you know, is the temple of the Holy Spirit, who is in you since you received him from God. You are not your own property; you have been bought and paid for. (1 Co. 6:19–20)

We are only the earthenware jars that hold this treasure to make it clear that such an overwhelming power comes from God and not from us. (2 Co. 4:7)

You have stripped off your old behavior with your old self, and you have put on a new self which will progress toward true knowledge the more it is renewed in the image of its creator . . . There is only Christ: he is everything and he is in everything. (Col. 3:9–11)

I live now not with my own life but with the life of Christ who lives in me. (Ga. 2:20)

Whoever keeps his commandments
lives in God and God lives in him.
We know that he lives in us
by the Spirit he has given us. (1 Jn. 3:24)

He who eats my flesh and drinks my blood
lives in me
and I live in him. (Jn. 6:56)

———❦———

## *For Further Reflection*

Life to me, of course, is Christ. (Ph. 1:21)

If anyone loves me he will keep my word,
and my Father will love him,
and we shall come to him
and make our home with him. (Jn. 14:23)

Examine yourselves to make sure you are in the faith; test yourselves. Do you acknowledge that Jesus Christ is really in you? (2 Co. 13:5)

# 20

# SERVANTHOOD

So often we look for the heroic, the difficult, the grandiose when it comes to serving one another. We fantasize how well we would do a particularly difficult task, how faithful we would be, how available and open to God's people. Yet servanthood within the Christian community has little to do with heroics, and everything to do with the nitty-gritty routine of placing the other person ahead of us in all things.

Jesus, of course, gives us the best example when he washed the feet of the disciples. He stooped low in order to serve them. In fact, he was upset when Peter did not want him to be the servant. Yet Jesus persisted; he had to serve in order to be true to his identity as the Son of God. We too must serve in order to be true to our identity as believers in the Son of God, and children of the Father.

The service we offer, therefore, is meant to take ordinary forms: housework, schoolwork, our job, being available to another, offering our time freely, performing a task willingly without grumbling, etc. This is the servanthood that marks a believer. This is the servanthood that marked the Lord's ministry, and continues to mark his ministry as he serves us in the power of his Spirit.

## Scripture Verses

Each one of you has received a special grace, so, like good stewards responsible for all these different graces of God, put yourselves at the service of others. (1 Pt. 4:10)

Let us be concerned for each other, to stir a response in love and good works. (Heb. 10:24)

And to some, his gift was that they should be apostles; to some, prophets; to some, evangelists; to some, pastors and teachers; so that the saints together make a unity in the work of service. (Ep. 4:11–12)

The personal requirements for effective servanthood. (1 Tm. 3:1–3)

People must think of us as Christ's servants, stewards entrusted with the mysteries of God. What is expected of stewards is that each one should be found worthy of his trust. (1 Co. 4:1–2)

"Do you understand," he [Jesus] said, "what I have done to you? You call me Master and Lord, and rightly; so I am. If I, then, the Lord and Master, have washed your feet, you should wash each other's feet. I have given you an example so that you may copy what I have done to you." (Jn. 13:12–15)

Anyone who wants to be great among you must be your servant, and anyone who wants to be first among you must be your slave, just as the Son of Man came not to be served but to serve, and to give his life as a ransom for many. (Mt. 20:26–28)

---

## For Further Reflection

[Jesus] is the living stone, rejected by men but chosen by God and precious to him; set yourselves close to him, so that you too, the holy priesthood that offers the spiritual sacrifices which Jesus Christ has made acceptable to God, may be living stones making a spiritual house. (1 Pt. 2:4–5)

Now you together are Christ's body . . . in the Church. God has given the first place to apostles, the second to prophets, the third to teachers; after these, miracles, and after them the gift of healing; helpers, good leaders, those with many languages . . .

You must want love more than anything else; but still hope for the spiritual gifts as well. (1 Co. 12:28–14:1)

Be the shepherds of the flock of God that is entrusted to you: watch over it, not simply as a duty but gladly, because God wants it; not for sordid money, but because you are eager to do it. Never be a dictator over any group that is put in your charge. (1 Pt. 5:1–3)

# 21

# LOVER AND SPOUSE

When I think of a lover, I think of someone who is kind, gentle, and considerate. Someone who has my best interests at heart. Someone who lifts me up, bringing the best out of me: someone who "breathes with me" while allowing me to be myself; someone who loves me into being, in a sense, whose presence creates me, whose absence dismays me.

Though such a description might aptly apply to a human lover, it also applies to God, the lover par excellence. He is the one whose very presence loves us into being; he is the one whose absence breaks the heart with longing sighs; he is the one who desires to embrace us, caress us, enrich us, and make us his own.

As lover and spouse God has taken us as his very own, and allowed us to enter into the very depths of his being. In addition, he has allowed us to hold him in the depths of our being. In this way we are one—together—as lovers should be.

Allow yourself the privilege and experience of feeling God's love for you. Do not be afraid of the emotions at a time like this. Since he is our lover and spouse, we should be open to all the normal relations and feelings that lovers and spouses would have as part of their experiences. Let it be that way with God.

## Scripture Verses

I will betroth you to myself for ever,
betroth you with integrity and justice,

with tenderness and love;
I will betroth you to myself with faithfulness,
and you will come to know Yahweh. (Ho. 2:21–22)


Listen, daughter, pay careful attention:
forget your nation and your ancestral home,
then the king will fall in love with your beauty.
He is your master now, bow down to him. (Ps. 45:10–11)


Let us be glad and joyful and give praise to God, because this is
the time for the marriage of the Lamb. His bride is ready, and
she has been able to dress herself in dazzling white linen, because her linen is made of the good deeds of the saints.
(Rv. 19:7–8)


Christ loved the Church and sacrificed himself for her to make
her holy. He made her clean by washing her in water with a
form of words, so that when he took her to himself she would
be glorious, with no speck or wrinkle or anything like that, but
holy and faultless. (Ep. 5:25–27)


Set me like a seal on your heart,
like a seal on your arm.
For love is strong as Death,
jealousy relentless as Sheol.
The flash of it is a flash of fire,
a flame of Yahweh himself
Love no flood can quench
no torrents drown. (Sg. 8:6–7)

Like a young man marrying a virgin,
so will the one who built you wed you,
and as the bridegroom rejoices in his bride,
so will your God rejoice in you. (Is. 62:5)


I am my Beloved's,
and his desire is for me.
Come, my Beloved,
let us go to the fields . . .
Then I shall give you the gift of my love. (Sg. 7:11–13)


&#10070;


## *For Further Reflection*

He has taken me to his banquet hall,
and the banner he raises over me is love . . .
His left arm is under my head,
his right embraces me. (Sg. 2:4–6)


Now your creator will be your husband,
his name, Yahweh Sabaoth, . . .
he is called the God of the whole earth. (Is. 54:5)


You are wholly beautiful, my love,
and without blemish.
Come . . . my promised bride,
. . . come on your way . . .
You ravish my heart,
with a single one of your glances. (Sg. 4:7–9)

# 22

# REALITY OF OUR SINFULNESS

To acknowledge sin is to acknowledge a reality. The fact is that humankind continually refuses to accept the gift of the Father —the gift of sonship/daughtership which he lavishes on us through the reconciling ministry of his Son, Jesus. This gift of sonship/daughtership gives us life, true life, yet we continually refuse it.

We refuse the gift by seeking our identity, our very self, outside the reality of the Father's love. We seek to know ourselves, and be ourselves through our own power rather than coming to know ourselves and be ourselves through the creative power of God who created us in his image and likeness. Sin, therefore, is standing outside the creative exchange of love and identity which the Father offers to us in Jesus. It is standing on our own, rather than standing in him. It is standing apart from reality while we live in our own unreality.

Jesus has come to show us the way to be real. He has come to show us what it means to be ourselves. He has come to show us what it means to be child of God. He is sinless because he acknowledged and accepted all these gifts from the Father. We remain sinners each time we seek these gifts of identity and being from anyone other than the Lord.

## Scripture Verses

The Fall. (Gn. 3:1–24)

There is not a good man left, no, not one;
there is not one who understands,
not one who looks for God.
All have turned aside, tainted all alike. (Rm. 3:10–12)

Sin entered the world through one man, and through sin death,
and thus death has spread through the whole human race because everyone has sinned. (Rm. 5:12)

Men have shown they prefer
darkness to the light
because their deeds were evil.
And indeed, everybody who does wrong
hates the light and avoids it. (Jn. 3:19–20)

You know I was born guilty,
a sinner from the moment of conception. (Ps. 51:5)

If we say we have no sin in us,
we are deceiving ourselves
and refusing to admit the truth. (1 Jn. 1:8)

I have been sold as a slave to sin . . . I find myself doing the very things I hate . . . with the result that instead of doing the good things I want to do, I carry out the sinful things I do not want. (Rm. 7:14–19)

---∞---

## For Further Reflection

We ought, then, to turn our minds more attentively than before to what we have been taught . . . we shall certainly not go unpunished if we neglect this salvation that is promised to us. (Heb. 2:1–3)

He who is not with me is against me, and he who does not gather with me scatters. (Mt. 12:30)

O Lord, God great and to be feared, you keep the covenant and have kindness for those who love you and keep your commandments: we have sinned, we have done wrong, we have acted wickedly, . . . and turned away. (Dt. 9:4–5)

# 23

# THE POWER OF THE CROSS

Since the cross of Jesus is the perfect example of true dying to self and giving oneself to another, it is easy to understand why sin and death are destroyed in its embrace. Evil can only exist where there is self-centeredness, where a person uses someone for gain, no matter how inconsequential the matter. By offering himself freely and without compromise, however, Jesus revealed himself to the Evil One as an individual who was totally for the other. To the Evil One this was incomprehensible. In trying to cling to Jesus, therefore, in trying to feed on him, Evil discovered that it had nothing on which to hold. It found itself, therefore, unable to exist in Jesus; it was seen for what it really is, "no-thing" in Jesus. Within the embrace of such total self-giving, Evil was not able to live.

On the cross, therefore, we are able to join ourselves to Jesus, who totally destroyed the domain and power of Evil. By our remaining in the Lord, evil cannot remain in us, since it has nothing to feed on, or cling to, for in Jesus only good can exist.

## Scripture Verses

[Jesus] has overridden the Law, and canceled every record of the debt that we had to pay; he has done away with it by nailing it to the cross. (Col. 2:14)

He was bearing our faults in his own body on the cross, so that we might die to our faults and live for holiness; through his wounds you have been healed. (1 Pt. 2:24)

Remember, the ransom that was paid to free you from the useless way of life your ancestors handed down was not paid in anything corruptible, neither in silver nor gold, but in the precious blood of a lamb without spot or stain, namely Christ. (1 Pt. 1:18–19)

The language of the cross may be illogical to those who are not on the way to salvation, but those of us who are on the way see it as God's power to save . . . for God's foolishness is wiser than human wisdom, and God's weakness is stronger than human strength. (1 Co. 1:18–25)

He made peace
by his death on the cross. (Col. 1:20)

Through Jesus' cross and resurrection, we are able to live and reign in him. (2 Tm. 2:8–13)

[Jesus] became as men are;
and being as all men are,
he was humbler yet,
even to accepting death,
death on a cross.
But God raised him on high . . .
so that every tongue should acclaim
Jesus Christ as Lord. (Ph. 2:7–11)

---

## For Further Reflection

The Son of Man must be lifted up
as Moses lifted up the serpent in the desert,
so that everyone who believes may have eternal life in him.
(Jn. 3:13–15)


The cross of Christ restores peace between the Jew and the
pagan. (Ep. 2:13–16)


[God meant us] to win salvation through our Lord Jesus Christ,
who died for us so that, alive or dead, we should still live united
to him. (1 Th. 5:9–10)

# 24

# TRUSTING GOD'S CARE FOR US

Perhaps a good way to get the feel of these passages is to do precisely what the scripture says: "Look at the flowers growing in the fields." By looking at the beauty around us, and realizing that it is we who are God's children, it might be easier to live and believe the reality of faith that the scripture offers us in these passages.

Trusting God's care for us, however, does not give us license to ignore our basic responsibility as human beings. We are meant to cooperate with the Lord by showing one another the same care he offers us. In many instances, for example, we are called to be channels of his care and concern. He does not usually operate within a vacuum, but expects us to work with him as he provides for all our needs and the needs of our brothers and sisters.

Finally, realize also that the Lord's promise is to provide for our needs, not necessarily our wants. There is a difference. Pray, therefore, that this time with the Lord will help you discover what that difference is for you. Then, thank him for providing for your every need.

## Scripture Verses

Commit your fate to Yahweh,
trust in him and he will act . . .
Be quiet before Yahweh, and wait patiently for him.
(Ps. 37:5–7)

Trust wholeheartedly in Yahweh,
put no faith in your own perception;
in every course you take, have him in mind:
he will see that your paths are smooth. (Pr. 3:5–6)


See now, he is the God of my salvation
I have trust now and no fear,
for Yahweh is my strength, my song,
he is my salvation. (Is. 12:2)


Do not be afraid, for I am with you;
stop being anxious . . . for I am your God.
I give you strength, I bring you help . . .
I am holding you by the right hand. (Is. 41:10–13)


Yahweh is my shepherd,
I lack nothing . . .
To the waters of repose he leads me;
there he revives my soul . . . (Ps. 23)


I put my trust in you;
in God, whose word I praise.
in God I put my trust, fearing nothing;
what can men do to me? (Ps. 56:3–4)


That is why I am telling you not to worry about your life
. . . Look at the birds in the sky . . . the flowers growing in
the fields . . . will he not look much more after you . . . ?
(Mt. 6:25–30)

## *For Further Reflection*

Yahweh is my rock and my bastion,
my deliverer is my God
I take shelter in him, my rock . . .
my stronghold and my refuge . . .
on Yahweh I call
and am saved from my enemies. (Ps. 18:2)


Trust in Yahweh for ever,
for Yahweh is the everlasting Rock;
he has brought low those who lived high up. (Is. 26:4–5)


Unload all your worries onto him, since he is looking after you.
(1 Pt. 5:7)

# 25

# GOD'S COVENANT WITH HIS PEOPLE

The marvel of God's covenant with his people is that he reveals through his relationship with us how we are called to relate to one another, namely, by loving unilaterally; offering ourselves with no questions asked; taking the other to ourselves while allowing him/her the freedom to be whom he/she chooses to be. This is covenant.

The covenant that God has made with his people shows us what it means to be one with someone, yet remaining distinct from that person. This is, of course, symbolized most explicitly in the Sacrament of Marriage where two become one, though each remains distinct. This is covenant.

God's covenant with us is, of course, enfleshed in the person of Jesus Christ, whose unilateral love led him to the cross. In offering us love in Jesus, the Father will never hold back his love because we may or may not have responded. His love is not contingent upon ours. This is covenant.

## Scripture Verses

You are a people consecrated to Yahweh your God . . . It was for love of you that Yahweh . . . redeemed you from the house of slavery . . . Know then that Yahweh your God is God indeed, the faithful God who is true to his covenant. (Dt. 7:6–9)

He brings a new covenant, as the mediator, only so that the people who were called to an eternal inheritance may actually receive what was promised: his death took place to cancel the sins that infringed the earlier covenant. (Heb. 9:15)

See the days are coming . . . when I will make a new covenant with the House of Israel . . . Deep within them I will plant my Law, writing it on their hearts. Then I will be their God and they shall be my people . . . They will all know me, the least no less than the greatest . . . since I will forgive their iniquity and never call their sin to mind. (Jr. 31:31–34)

You are a chosen race . . . a people set apart . . . Once you were not a people at all and now you are the People of God. (1 Pt. 2:9–10)

Through the blood of Jesus we have the right to enter the sanctuary, by a new way which he has opened for us, a living opening through the curtain, that is to say, his body. (Heb. 10:19–20)

I will make an everlasting covenant with them; I will not cease in my efforts for their good. (Jr. 32:40)

My covenant of peace with you will never be shaken. (Is. 54:10)

## *For Further Reflection*

You yourselves have seen what I did with the Egyptians, how I carried you on eagle's wings and brought you to myself. From this you know that now, if you obey my voice and hold fast to my covenant, you of all the nations shall be my very own for all the earth is mine. I will count you a kingdom of priests, a consecrated nation. (Ex. 19:4–6)

But now in Christ Jesus, you that used to be so far apart from us have been brought very close, by the blood of Christ. (Ep. 2:13)

Remember Yahweh your God: it was he who gave you this strength and won you this power, thus keeping the covenant then as today, that he swore to your fathers. (Dt. 8:18)

# 26

# LIVE IN CHRIST JESUS

To live in Christ Jesus is to live in reality; all else is borderline. He alone, the Crucified One raised from the dead, is truly alive and real because he alone, and those who abide in him, exist in the Father with the Spirit thereby echoing the trinitarian model of relationship and life.

It is the Father who offers all that he is to the Son, freely and unconditionally; it is the Son, the Word, who receives all that is offered, acknowledging the Father who is the Giver. What the Word receives is the gift of Sonship; what he returns to the Father is the acceptance that God is Father, Giver of all. All this takes place with the Spirit, the eternal bond of exchange what always was, is, and will be for he is God.

Living in Jesus is to live in this trinitarian exchange, this eternal reality where all is given, all is accepted, and all is celebrated and shared. In such an environment we can see how life really is.

## Scripture Verses

You have been taught that when we were baptized in Christ Jesus we were baptized into his death; . . . we went into the tomb with him and joined him in death, so that as Christ was raised from the dead by the Father's glory, we too might live a new life . . . you too must consider yourselves to be . . . alive for God in Christ Jesus. (Rm. 6:3–11)

In his body lives the fullness of divinity, and in him you too find your own fulfillment. *(See* Col. 2:9–13)

And for anyone who is in Christ, there is a new creation. *(See* Co. 5:14–21)

In your minds you must be the same as Christ Jesus.
(Ph. 2:1–11)

Since you have been brought back to true life with Christ you must look for the things that are in heaven . . . not on the things that are on the earth. *(See* Col. 3:1–4)

You must live your whole life . . . rooted in him, and built on him. (2 Tm. 2:11–12)

I live now not with my own life but with the life of Christ who lives in me. (Ga. 2:20)

---

## For Further Reflection

But God loved us with so much love . . . that he brought us to life with Christ . . . and gave us a place with him . . . in Christ Jesus. (Ep. 2:4–6)

You are, all of you, sons of God through faith in Christ Jesus. All baptized in Christ, you have all clothed yourselves in Christ, and there are no more distinctions . . . but all of you are one in Christ Jesus. (Ga. 3:26–28)

Yes, but he was crucified through weakness, and still he lives now through the power of God. So then, we are weak, as he was, but we shall live with him, through the power of God. (2 Co. 13:4)

# 27

# OBEDIENCE

In today's society, obedience has a negative connotation. To be obedient often implies slavery, oppression, loss of freedom, etc. Scripturally, however, this is not the case.

Obedience, in its root meaning, is meant to communicate the notion of listening—more than just a haphazard listening, however. It indicates a straining to hear, a silent attentiveness that motivates our actions. A helpful image is one of two lovers in joyful embrace, straining to hear the other's sighs, rejoicing when words of love are spoken, and responding to the other's every request and movement. That is obedience.

Obedience, therefore, is a stance we take while facing the Beloved. We stand ready to hear and respond, not because one is master and one is servant, but because one is Lover and one is loved.

## Scripture Verses

It is not those who say to me, "Lord, Lord," who will enter the kingdom of heaven, but the person who does the will of my Father in heaven. (Mt. 7:21)


When you have done all you have been told to do, say, "We are merely servants: we have done no more than our duty." *(See* Lk. 17:7–10)

My food
is to do the will of the one who sent me,
and to complete his work. (Jn. 4:34)


Let your heart treasure what I have to say,
keep my principles and you shall live; . . .
never deviate from my words. (Pr. 4:4–5)


Everyone who listens to these words of mine and acts on them
will be like the sensible man who built his house on rock.
*(See* Mt. 7:21–27)


If anyone loves me he will keep my word. (Jn. 14:23)


Now as he was speaking, a woman in the crowd raised her
voice and said, "Happy the womb that bore you and the breasts
you sucked!" But he replied, "Still happier those who hear the
word of God and keep it!" (Lk. 11:27–28)

———————⋙———————

## *For Further Reflection*

My son, do not forget my teaching,
let your heart keep my principles,
for these will give you lengthier days,
longer years of life, and greater happiness. (Pr. 3:1–2)

Mary's obedience to God's Word. (Lk. 1:26–28)

Why do you call me, "Lord, Lord" and not do what I say? . . . the one who listens and does nothing is like the man who built his house on soil, with no foundations. (Lk. 6:46–49)

# 28

# COST OF DISCIPLESHIP

Our culture has become very cost conscious. With inflation and high unemployment, we are constantly striving to get the most for our money. Bargains, sales, coupon clippings, etc., have become part of our life.

Even with our attempts to get the most for less, however, we still find that sacrifice and savings are often needed to obtain the most desirable items. Once our heart is set on such an item, a car for example, do we not save, doing without in some areas so that we can have the item we desire?

So it is with discipleship. Yes, it costs, but it is the most desirable of all possessions. We willingly pay the price for things that are not going to last: a car, the best designer clothes, a house; and we willingly pay the price for items which we need in order to live: food, medicine, shelter. Yet with the cost of discipleship, the cost of following the Lord, we try to haggle and compromise and bargain. It cannot be.

It should not surprise us that discipleship costs so much. Valuables usually do. The question we need to ask is whether we are willing to pay the price. In answering that question, remember that Love has paid a price for us.

## Scripture Verses

If anyone wants to be a follower of mine, let him renounce himself and take up his cross and follow me. For anyone who wants to save his life will lose it; but anyone who loses his life

for my sake, and for the sake of the gospel, will save it.
(Mk. 8:34–35)

I am the Way, the Truth and the Life.
No one can come to the Father except through me. (Jn. 14:6)

Enter by the narrow gate, since the road that leads to perdition is wide and spacious, and many take it; but it is a narrow gate and a hard road that leads to life, and only a few find it. (Mt. 7:13–14)

One of the scribes then came up and said to him, "Master, I will follow you wherever you go." Jesus replied, "Foxes have holes and the birds of the air have nests, but the Son of Man has nowhere to lay his head." (Mt. 8:19)

If any man comes to me without hating his father, mother, wife, children, brothers, sisters, yes and his own life too, he cannot be my disciple. Anyone who does not carry his cross and come after me cannot be my disciple. (Lk. 14:26–27)

If you wish to be perfect, go and sell what you own and give the money to the poor, and you will have treasure in heaven; then come, follow me! (Mt. 19:21)

I believe nothing can happen that will outweigh the supreme advantage of knowing Christ Jesus my Lord. For him I have accepted the loss of everything, and I look on everything as so much rubbish if only I can have Christ. (Ph. 3:8)

———⊷⊶———

## *For Further Reflection*

You are my friends,
if you do what I command you. (Jn. 15:14)


When you were young
you put on your own belt,
and walked where you liked;
but when you grow old
you will stretch out your hands,
and somebody else will put a belt around you
and take you where you would rather not go. (Jn. 21:18)


He noticed a tax collector, Levi by name, sitting by the customs house, and said to him, "Follow me." And leaving everything he got up and followed him. (Lk. 5:27–28)

# 29

# TRIALS

Though we pretend, we seldom have an answer for everything. We wish we could answer every query with a neat response and explanation, yet it seldom works out that way no matter how hard we try.

In explaining trials or suffering, we spend hours trying to figure out the why and how of it all, but we proceed at a snail's pace. Better for us to open our hearts to all the Lord offers, asking him to show us how a particular trial can lead us closer to the reality of his love. Notice that our concern is not why another person is undergoing a difficulty, but how we can grow through the trial and difficulty we are undergoing. How another is called to respond, or why another is called to respond in a particular way is not our concern.

As believers, we know that everything is gift, and that all of God's gifts are meant, in some way, to lead us to him. This is also true for any trials we undergo. He only sends us those which are going to lead us closer to him. Ask not why, therefore, we are undergoing a trial. We know why—to move closer to him.

## Scripture Verses

Can you drink the cup that I am going to drink? (Mt. 20:22)

Unless a wheat grain falls on the ground and dies,
it remains only a single grain; . . .
Anyone who loves his life loses it; . . .
If a man serves me, he must follow me. (Jn. 12:24–26)

Happy the man who stands firm when trials come. He has
proved himself and will win the prize of life, the crown that the
Lord has promised to those who love him. (Jm. 1:12)

Though this outer man of ours may be falling into decay, the
inner man is renewed day by day. Yes, the troubles . . . train
us for the carrying of a weight of eternal glory which is out of
all proportion to them. (2 Co. 4:16–17)

You may . . . have to bear being plagued by all sorts of trials;
so that, when Jesus Christ is revealed, your faith will have been
tested . . . and then you will have praise and glory and honor.
(1 Pt. 1:6–7)

You will always have your trials, but when they come, try to treat them as a happy privilege; you understand that your faith is only put to the test to make you patient. (Jm. 1:2–3)

The trials that you have had to bear are not more than people normally have. You can trust God not to let you be tried beyond your strength, and with any trial he will give you a way out of it and the strength to bear it. (1 Co. 10:13)

———❦———

## For Further Reflection

If anyone wants to be a follower of mine, let him renounce himself and take up his cross and follow me. (Mk. 8:34)

And if we are children we are heirs as well: heirs of God and coheirs with Christ, sharing his sufferings so as to share his glory. (Rm. 8:17)

If we hold firm then we shall reign with him. (2 Tm. 2:1–13)

# 30

# I HAVE LOVED YOU WITH AN EVERLASTING LOVE

In a world where people find it difficult to say "forever," it is hard for us to grasp the concept of everlasting love. This occurs because we are trying to be rational and logical about something which is irrational and passionate. Better to be grasped by it than to try and grasp it.

Look at the signs of God's passionate madness: He sent his Son to die for our sins; he offers us forgiveness in an unconditional way; he allows us to be his sons and daughters; he blesses us with creation, with life, with breath; he sends us his Spirit so we can experience his love now; he makes us in his image and likeness so that our very center rests in his divinity. This is love everlasting. This is the love which we cannot grasp, but which grasps us in Jesus the Lord.

## Scripture Verses

I have loved you with an everlasting love,
so I am constant in my affection for you. (Jr. 31:3)


But now, thus says Yahweh . . .
Do not be afraid, for I have redeemed you;
I have called you by your name, you are mine . . .
Do not be afraid, for I am with you. (Is. 43:1–5)

Does a woman forget her baby at the breast,
or fail to cherish the son of her womb?
Yet even if these forget,
I will never forget you.
See, I have branded you on the palm of my hands,
Your ramparts are always under my eye. (Is. 49:15–16)


Deep within them I will plant my Law, writing it on their
hearts. Then I will be their God and they shall be my people
. . . they will all know me, the least no less than the greatest.
(Jr. 31:33–34)


What proves that God loves us is that Christ died for us while
we were still sinners. (Rm. 5:7)

## Washing of the Feet
Jesus . . . had always loved those who were his . . . but now
he showed how perfect his love was. (Jn. 13:1–15)


Think of the love that the Father has lavished on us,
by letting us be called God's children. (1 Jn. 3:1–2)

## *For Further Reflection*

Yahweh, you examine me and know me . . .
when I was being formed in secret,
knitted together in the limbo of the womb. (Ps. 139:1–15)


I am going to look after my flock myself and keep all of it in
view . . . I myself will show them where to rest . . . I shall
be a true shepherd to them. (Ez. 34:11–16)


Yes, God loved the world so much,
that he gave his only Son,
so that everyone who believes in him may not be lost
but may have eternal life. *(See* Jn. 3:16–18)

# 31

# THE PROMISED REDEEMER

It is the Christmas Story which summarizes the hopes of humankind, for it is here, in the simple story of one born in a cave, that we realize how uncomplicated the answer really is. There is little need for us to become entwined with "solutions" that seem to create more problems than they solve; there is little reason for us to become entangled with "slogans" that stir our sensibilities yet produce few results; there is little need for us to take the weight of the world upon our shoulders, as if all creation were dependent on our ability to accomplish a task or a function.

Yes, it is in the Christmas Story that all of this is placed in the proper perspective—an essential simplicity which speaks of love offered through Jesus, and love protected and nurtured through Mary and Joseph.

For many generations the world awaited this Redeemer. In the hearts of all there was a yearning to re-establish that which was missing. Oh yes, it is true that many did not identify the yearning as such, but it was there nonetheless, expressed in many different ways. And so it happened: that which was promised from the beginning became the Beginning. Jesus, the love of the Father, the tangible presence of the Spirit who is love, became one with us.

The promise, however, is not complete. More is yet to come, for the promise is one of eternal love which can never be completely expended. And so it continues. The promise remains, beckoning us to experience love in the simplicity of the Christmas Story, in the simplicity of love given and love received.

## Scripture Verses

A shoot springs from the stock of Jesse,
a scion thrusts from his roots:
on him the spirit of Yahweh rests,
a spirit of wisdom and insight,
a spirit of counsel and power,
a spirit of knowledge and of the fear of Yahweh. (Is. 11:1–2)


See, the days are coming—it is Yahweh who speaks—
when I will raise a virtuous Branch for David,
who will reign as true king and be wise,
practicing honesty and integrity in the land.
In his days Judah will be saved
and Israel dwell in confidence.
And this is the name he will be called:
Yahweh-our-integrity. (Jr. 23:5–6)


The Lord himself, therefore,
will give you a sign.
It is this: the maiden is with child
and will soon give birth to a son
whom she will call Immanuel. (Is. 7:14)


[Yahweh says]
It is not enough for you to be my servant,

to restore the tribes of Jacob and bring back the survivors of
    Israel;
I will make you the light of the nations
so that my salvation may reach to the ends of the earth.
(Is. 49:6)


But you, (Bethlehem) Ephrathah,
the least of the clans of Judah,
out of you will be born for me
the one who is to rule over Israel:
his origin goes back to the distant past,
to the days of old . . .
He will stand and feed his flock
with the power of Yahweh,
with the majesty of the name of his God. (Mi. 5:1–3)


[Yahweh says] I am going to look after my flock myself and
keep all of it in view . . . I mean to raise up one shepherd, my
servant David, . . . he will pasture them, and be their shepherd. (Ez. 34:11–23)


[the angel said to Mary:] Rejoice, so highly favored! The Lord is
with you . . . You are to conceive and bear a son, and you
must name him Jesus. He will be great and will be called Son of
the Most High . . . he will rule over the House of Jacob for
ever and his reign will have no end. *(See* Lk. 1:26–38;)

## *For Further Reflection*

The scepter shall not pass from Judah,
nor the mace from between his feet,
until he comes to whom it belongs,
to whom the peoples shall render obedience. (Gn. 49:10)


A little while now, and I am going to shake the heavens and the earth, the sea and the dry land . . . and I will fill this Temple with glory, says Yahweh Sabaoth. (Hg. 2:6–9)


I know the plans I have in mind for you—it is Yahweh who speaks—plans for peace, not disaster, reserving a future full of hope for you. (Jr. 29:11–12)

# 32

# NEW LIFE

Born again! The phrase has recently become part of our church vocabulary, especially within the Charismatic Renewal experience which has touched thousands of people. This succinct phrase manages to convey many images: new life, new beginnings, a new start, rebirth. Yet the experience itself cannot really be summarized in a phrase of any length.

It is the reality of Jesus who enters our life which gives us the opportunity to be "born again": to be reborn into the reality of love which is the Father's presence to us in the Spirit. It is the opportunity to leave behind that which is false within ourselves, and receive in its place a new identity of life with Jesus. This is to be "born again."

Nicodemus, among others, did not understand how it could be. How could an individual return to the womb and reemerge a new person? Such is the mystery of love. It should not take us by surprise, however, since we experience something similar within human relationships. Think, for example, of the times you were "reborn" by a love you cherished or encountered. Think of how you felt renewed in every part of your being; how things looked different: creation, people, work, etc. In a sense, you experienced a type of born-again experience. With the Lord, however, it is more. It is complete, eternal, indescribable.

For whom is this possible? For everyone who accepts Jesus. No one need be excluded.

## Scripture Verses

Blessed be God the Father of our Lord Jesus Christ, who in his great mercy has given us a new birth as his sons, by raising Jesus Christ from the dead, so that we have a sure hope and the promise of an inheritance that can never be spoiled or soiled and never fade away. (1 Pt. 1:3–5)

When we were baptized in Christ Jesus we were baptized in his death; . . . so that as Christ was raised from the dead by the Father's glory, we too might live a new life. (Rm. 6:3–4)

You must give up your old way of life; you must put aside your old self, . . . your mind must be renewed by a spiritual revolution so that you can put on the new self that has been created in God's way, in the goodness and holiness of the truth. (Ep. 4:22–24)

Get rid of all the old yeast, and make yourselves into a completely new batch of bread, unleavened as you are meant to be. (1 Co. 5:7–8)

But when the kindness and love of God our savior for mankind were revealed, . . . it was for no reason except his own compassion that he saved us, by the cleansing water of rebirth and by renewing us with the Holy Spirit. (Tt. 3:4–5)

I tell you most solemnly,
unless a man is born through water and the Spirit,
he cannot enter the kingdom of God; . . .
Do not be surprised when I say:
You must be born from above. (Jn. 3:3–8)

If you have really died with Christ to the principles of this world, why do you still let rules dictate to you, as though you were still living in the world . . . Since you have been brought back to true life with Christ, you must look for the things that are in heaven. (*See* Col. 2:20–3:4)

---

## *For Further Reflection*

You have been buried with him, when you were baptized; and by baptism, too, you have been raised up with him . . . he has brought you to life with him. (Col. 2:9–12)

But God loved us with so much love that he was generous with his mercy: when we were dead through our sins, he brought us to life with Christ. (Ep. 2:4–5)

[Jesus's] life now is life with God; . . . you too must consider yourselves to be dead to sin but alive for God in Christ Jesus. (*See* Rm. 6:8–11)

# 33

# OUR MISSION

We all want to accomplish something. Our natural American tendency is to perform, to function, to succeed, to do. And so, it is quite easy to understand why those who follow the Lord automatically feel they must accomplish something in order to be a faithful follower. In fact, nothing could be farther from the truth.

The mission of Jesus, who is our example, gives us insight into this process. He did not set out to accomplish anything. He set out to be who he was, namely, Son of God, despite what others said to the contrary. His mission was one of being, in as full a way as possible, the person he really was, his true self. In doing this he accomplished redemption for all people. The accomplishment, however, came about because he was true to himself, not because of a task that was performed.

This is a difficult concept to understand since we are usually caught up with accomplishments rather than with being. It is even more difficult, however, for us to put it into practice, since it challenges us at our very roots—the level of being and identity rather than the objective level of accomplishment and function. Yet, the fact remains. Our mission as followers of Jesus is to be: to be him for others, to be children of the Father, to be brothers and sisters for one another. When we accept this, the accomplishments will follow.

## Scripture Verses

I have appointed you as sentry to the House of Israel. Whenever you hear a word from me, warn them in my Name. (Ez. 3:17)

Go, therefore, make disciples of all the nations; baptize them in the name of the Father and of the Son and of the Holy Spirit, and teach them to observe all the commands I gave you. (Mt. 28:19–20)

Life to me is not a thing to waste words on, provided that when I finish my race I have carried out the mission the Lord Jesus gave me—and that was to bear witness to the Good News of God's grace. (Ac. 20:24)

It is written that the Christ would suffer and on the third day rise from the dead, and that, in his name, repentance for the forgiveness of sins would be preached to all the nations, beginning from Jerusalem. You are witnesses to this. (Lk. 24:46–48)

We are ambassadors for Christ; it is as though God were appealing through us, and the appeal that we make in Christ's name is: be reconciled to God. (2 Co. 5:20)

The spirit of the Lord has been given to me,
for he has anointed me.
He has sent me to bring the good news to the poor,
to proclaim liberty to captives
and to the blind new sight,
to set the downtrodden free,
to proclaim the Lord's year of favor. (Lk. 4:18–19)


Proclaim that the kindgom of heaven is close at hand. Cure the
sick, raise the dead, cleanse the lepers, cast out devils. You
received without charge, give without charge . . . Remember,
I am sending you out like sheep among wolves; so be cunning as
serpents and yet as harmless as doves. (Mt. 10:7–16)

---

## For Further Reflection

After this the Lord appointed seventy-two others and sent
them out ahead of him, in pairs . . . I am sending you out like
lambs among wolves . . . [proclaiming] "The Kingdom of
God is very near." (Lk. 10:1–10)


Anyone who wants to become great among you must be your
servant, and anyone who wants to be first among you must be
slave to all. (Mk. 10:43–44)


The miraculous catch of fish symbolizes our mission.
(Jn. 21:1–6)

# 34

# FORGIVING OTHERS

The bridge which leads us to where we are going is forgiveness: the forgiveness we receive from the Father through Jesus, and the forgiveness we offer to one another in the Spirit. To ignore this in our lives, is to ignore the fact of God's love, for they spring from the same source, the same heart, the same God.

To be forgiven means we are no longer forced to carry the "extra baggage" that weighs us down. That weight may take the form of a scrupulous conscience, an angry verbal volley with a loved one, an unhealthy relationship with another, a lack of charity toward a neighbor, etc. It matters not, for forgiveness is always there.

Coupled with forgiveness, however, the stanchions which hold the bridge in place, is repentance. Here we may encounter some difficulty, since few people want to "repent." It sounds so harsh, so difficult, so humiliating. Yet, repentance, our willingness to change our life's direction, is needed if forgiveness is to be received. True, God always forgives, yet the process aborts unless repentance accompanies it. In a sense, our assurance of God's constant forgiveness gives us the confidence and impetus to repent so we can receive forgiveness.

During this period of prayer, therefore, realize how forgiveness and repentance are tied together. Then, having been instructed by the Spirit during the period of meditation, be ready to follow the directions he gives as he leads you to forgive others just as you have been forgiven.

## Scripture Verses

You have learned how it was said: You must love your neighbor and hate your enemy. But I say this to you: love your enemies and pray for those who persecute you. (Mt. 5:43–44)

If your brother does something wrong, go and have it out with him alone, between your two selves. (Mt. 18:15)

*Parable of the Unforgiving Debtor*
"You wicked servant," he said, "I canceled all that debt of yours when you appealed to me. Were you not bound then to have pity on your fellow servant just as I had pity on you?" *(See* Mt. 18:23–35)

If your brother does something wrong, reprove him and, if he is sorry, forgive him. And if he wrongs you seven times a day and seven times comes back to you and says, "I am sorry," you must forgive him. (Lk. 17:3–4)

[The disciples asked] "Lord, how often must I forgive my brother if he wrongs me? As often as seven times?" Jesus answered, "Not seven . . . but seventy-seven times." (Mt. 18:21–22)

When you stand in prayer, forgive whatever you have against anybody, so that your Father in heaven may forgive your failings too. (Mk. 11:25)

If you are bringing your offering to the altar and there remember that your brother has something against you, leave your offering there before the altar, go and be reconciled with your brother first, and then come back and present your offering. (Mt. 5:23–24)

---

## For Further Reflection

And forgive us our debts,
as we have forgiven those who are in debt to us.
*(See* Mt. 6:9–13)

Bear with one another; forgive each other as soon as a quarrel begins. (Col. 3:13)

If you do not forgive others, your heavenly Father will not forgive your failings either. (Mt. 6:15)

# 35

# FAITH

Faith is a way of perceiving reality, a way of standing in the world and relating to all of God's creation as he does. It comes as a gift from the Father, and is nurtured as we allow the Lord Jesus to be our eyes and our heart, as we allow his Spirit to be our soul and our breath, as we allow the Father to be our source and our life. This is faith—a stance that the world does not accept nor believe.

Faith, therefore, is more than doing things for God. It is a way of life, a way of living. Those who have been gifted with faith are called to live the life of Jesus, the life of death and resurrection, with all its implications, so that they can discover their root identity: sonship and daughtership. It is this relationship that allows us to be "justified," since here we now stand "upright" before the Lord; that is, we stand straight, not stooped or bent like slaves. We stand before him who has called us his own, before him who is God, who gives all and is all. Abraham knew what this meant as did the other people of faith mentioned in scripture. They knew that God was God and they were his. They were faith-filled people; men and women who received their life's identity from God who had gifted them with life.

The irony of it all is that God desires all humankind to be faith-filled, that is, to accept the life-giving stance of Jesus as the beginning and ending point of reality. Such a stand grounds us in the "really real" and offers us the possibility of touching reality.

## Scripture Verses

Jesus answered, "Have faith in God. I tell you solemnly, if anyone says to this mountain, Get up and throw yourself into the sea, with no hesitation in his heart but believing that what he says will happen, it will be done for him." (Mk. 11:22–23)

We acknowledge that what makes a man righteous is not obedience to the Law, but faith in Jesus Christ. (Ga. 2:16)

Without warning a storm broke over the lake . . . So they went to him . . . saying, "Save us, Lord, we are going down!" And he said to them, "Why are you so frightened, you men of little faith?" And with that he stood up and rebuked the wind and sea; and all was calm again. (Mt. 8:24–26)

I am the resurrection.
If anyone believes in me, even though he dies he will live
and whoever lives and believes in me
will never die.
Do you believe this? (Jn. 11:25–26)

For I am not ashamed of the Good News: it is the power of God saving all who have faith—Jews first, but Greeks as well— since this is what reveals the justice of God to us: it shows how

faith leads to faith, or as scripture says: The upright man finds
life through faith. (Rm. 1:16–17)

It is by grace that you have been saved, through faith; not by
anything of your own, but by a gift from God. (Ep. 2:8–9)

[Abraham] drew strength from faith and gave glory to God,
convinced that God had the power to do what he had promised.
*(See* Rm. 4:18–25)

———————— ∞ ————————

## *For Further Reflection*

Yahweh said to Abram, "Leave your country, your family,
and your father's house, for the land I will show you. I will
make you a great nation." (Gn. 12:1–2)

See how I lay in Zion
a stone of witness
a precious cornerstone, a foundation stone:
the believer shall not stumble. (Is. 28:16)

Both Jew and pagan sinned and forfeited God's glory, and both
are justified by the free gift of his grace by being redeemed in
Christ Jesus who was appointed by God to sacrifice his life so as
to win reconciliation through faith. (Rm. 3:23–25)

# 36

# THE PROMISED SPIRIT

I have always wanted to write in the style of William Shakespeare. I remember long hours laboring over his poems and plays trying to get the feel of the man, trying to capture his mind and spirit. In college, I majored in English so I could pursue this dream. I continued writing, yet never was able to approach his style and genius. Though I had read everything about him, and everything by him, I could not capture that for which I was seeking. Regardless of how hard I tried, I could not be him.

I have also wanted to be the type of person that Jesus is. Ever since childhood I have been mesmerized by his love and gentleness, his care and concern for others. I wanted to be just like him. And so, I read everything about him, hoping to find the secret ingredient which would enable me to capture his mind and spirit, which would enable me to be him. It was unlike my attempts with Shakespeare, because things were different: In studying about Jesus, I discovered that he wanted to give me his Spirit; he wanted to give me his mind and heart. In fact, I discovered that he actually sent his Spirit to those who desired to live in him.

You can imagine my excitement when I realized that such a feat was possible. At first I did not believe it could be so. After all, I had been sadly disappointed in my Shakespearean quest, despite all the hours of work and study. Now I learn that in Jesus the promise is already there for the asking. Why the difference? What would make it possible for Jesus to do this, yet impossible for Shakespeare?

The answer is simple. Jesus can fulfill his promises because he is alive. He is not distant from us, or dead, or gone, but alive—

able to do what he has promised to do. And he has promised us his Spirit, the Spirit who raised him from the dead, the Spirit which allowed him to say, "Abba," the Spirit who binds him to the Father. This is his promise already fulfilled for those who believe; this is the gift which is ours for the asking.

## Scripture Verses

When Pentecost day came around, they had all met in one room, when suddenly they heard what sounded like a powerful wind from heaven . . . and something appeared to them that seemed like tongues of fire; . . . they were all filled with the Holy Spirit. (Ac. 2:1–4)

When he [Jesus] had been at table with them, he had told them not to leave Jerusalem, but to wait there for what the Father had promised. "It is," he had said, "what you have heard me speak about: John baptized with water but you, not many days from now, will be baptized with the Holy Spirit." (Ac. 1:4–5)

I shall ask the Father,
and he will give you another Advocate
to be with you for ever,
that Spirit of truth
whom the world can never receive
since it neither sees nor knows him;
but you know him
because he is with you, he is in you. (Jn. 14:16–17)

When the apostles in Jerusalem heard that Samaria had accepted the word of God, they sent Peter and John to them, . . . and prayed for the Samaritans to receive the Holy Spirit, for as yet he had not come down on any of them . . . Then they laid hands on them, and they received the Holy Spirit. (Ac. 8:14–17)

If any man is thirsty, let him come to me!
Let the man come and drink who believes in me!
. . . He was speaking of the Spirit which those who believed in him were to receive. (Jn. 7:37–39)

The Spirit too comes to help us in our weakness. For when we cannot choose words to pray properly, the Spirit himself expresses our plea in a way that could never be put into words. (Rm. 8:26)

If you then . . . know how to give your children what is good, how much more will the heavenly Father give the Holy Spirit to those who ask him! (Lk. 11:13)

------◦◦◦------

## For Further Reflection

But the Advocate, the Holy Spirit,
whom the Father will send in my name
will teach you everything
and remind you of all I have said to you. (Jn. 14:26)

Remember it is God himself who assures us all, and you, of our standing in Christ, and has anointed us, marking us with his seal and giving us the pledge, the Spirit, that we carry in our hearts. (2 Co. 1:21–22)


Empowered by the Spirit we are a changed people. (Ac. 19:1–7)

# 37

# SUFFERING

There was a popular song sung not too long ago in which Carly Simon mourned: "Suffering was the only thing that made me feel I was alive." Without realizing it, she was expressing a reality which offers us insight into the reason for human suffering, and the reason for Jesus's suffering on the cross.

When we look at our experience, and the experience of others, we can honestly say that all people do not experience the exact same things: some are happy, while others are sad; some are rich, while others are poor; some are despondent, while others are joyful. In fact, there is nothing which all humanity experiences as one except, perhaps, suffering. That alone seems to be part and parcel of our humanity. Rich or poor, sad or happy, all seem to encounter suffering at some time of their life. It may be the suffering that comes from persecution, or the loss of a loved one. It may be the suffering that stems from a disease, or from plans gone awry. In a sense, suffering is the common denominator of our humanity.

We know that Jesus, in desiring to be one with us in all things, took upon himself all that we are. In doing so, he also accepted suffering lest he be dispensed from that very experience which we share together. And so he suffered in the same ways that we suffer—even to the point of death. In this way he was truly able to be one with us and one like us.

Suffering, therefore, is that part of reality which is identified with our very humanity. The proof that it is part of our humanity is seen in Jesus the one who is totally and completely human. In his suffering he showed us what it means to be fully alive and human, so we might receive consolation in our times of suffering, knowing he has paved the way for us, through suffering, into the fullness of life.

## Scripture Verses

Suffering is part of your training. God is treating you as his sons . . . So hold up your limp arms and steady your trembling knees . . . the injured limb will not be wrenched, it will grow strong again. (Heb. 12:7–13)

[the Lord has said] "My grace is enough for you: my power is at its best in weakness." So I shall be very happy to make my weakness my special boast . . . I am quite content with my weaknesses . . . and the agonies I go through for Christ's sake. (2 Co. 12:9–10)

All I want is to know Christ and the power of his resurrection and to share his sufferings by reproducing the pattern of his death. (Ph. 3:10)

I think that what we suffer in this life can never be compared to the glory, as yet unrevealed, which is waiting for us. (Rm. 8:18)

Be calm but vigilant, because your enemy the devil is prowling around like a roaring lion, looking for someone to eat. Stand up to him, strong in faith and in the knowledge that your brothers all over the world are suffering the same things. You will have to suffer only for a little while: the God of all grace who called you to eternal glory in Christ will see that all is well again: he will confirm, strengthen and support you. (1 Pt. 5:8–10)

Come to me, all you who labor and are overburdened, and I will give you rest. Shoulder my yoke and learn from me, for I am gentle and humble in heart, and you will find rest for your souls. Yes, my yoke is easy and my burden light. (Mt. 11:28–30)

It would be a sign from God that he has given you the privilege not only of believing in Christ, but of suffering for him as well. (Ph. 1:28–29)

❧

# For Further Reflection

Blessed be the God and Father of our Lord Jesus Christ . . . who comforts us in all our sorrows, so that we can offer others, in their sorrows, the consolation that we have received from God ourselves. Indeed, as the sufferings of Christ overflow to us, so, through Christ, does our consolation overflow. (2 Co. 1:3–5)

We can boast about our sufferings. These sufferings bring patience, as we know, and patience brings perseverance, and perseverance brings hope. (Rm. 5:3–4)

If you do have to suffer . . . count it a blessing. (1 Pt. 3:14)

# 38

# GOD HEALS HIS PEOPLE

The scriptures are filled with stories of healings. Again and again the evangelists recount the times when the sick came to the Lord seeking wholeness in him. In times past, many of these accounts were thought to be "myths" which never really occurred. In fact, there was a time in our Church when the healing power of Jesus was downplayed and demythologized to such a degree that the healing stories were either ignored or considered to be later additions to the Gospel texts.

Today, however, feelings have begun to change. With the advent of the charismatic movement within the Church, and the restoration of the Sacrament of Anointing of the Sick, our consciousness is gradually being raised regarding the possibility and the desirability of being healed in the name of Jesus.

This healing power, so powerfully exhibited at our Church's Marian shrines, as well as through the Sacraments of the Church, reveal to us the depth of God's love and power present within his people. Jesus himself reminds us that we will do greater things than he. Healing, therefore, being one of the services he offered the people, should be anticipated as part of our Church's experience.

A key word, of course, is anticipated. We might easily accept or expect God to work for and through someone else, but we hesitate to claim or anticipate that he might work for and through us. Yet, the power of healing belongs to us as Church, not just to one special individual or "healer." Do not, therefore, be afraid if and when the Lord leads you to pray for the release of his healing power. He intends it to be manifested for his glory and honor.

Will all be healed? In the Kingdom all will be healed; here on earth, when we pray for healing, we can expect that the process will, at the very least, begin to take place. For some it will culminate here for all to see. For others, it will continue into eternity so that all may be whole in Jesus.

## Scripture Verses

If one of you is ill, he should send for the elders of the church, and they must anoint him with oil in the name of the Lord and pray over him. The prayer of faith will save the sick man. (Jm. 5:14–15)

*Cure of the Centurion's Servant*
Just give the word and my servant will be cured.
*(See* Mt. 8:5–13)

*The Blind Man at Jericho*
Jesus spoke, "What do you want me to do for you?" The blind man said to him, "Master, let me see again." Jesus said to him, "Go; your faith has saved you." And immediately his sight returned. *(See* Mk. 10:46–52)

*Cure of a Leper*
"Sir," he [the leper] said, "if you want to, you can cure me." Jesus stretched out his hand, touched him and said, "Of course I want to! Be cured!" *(See* Lk. 5:12–16)

*Cure of the Woman with a Hemorrhage*
"If I can only touch his cloak I shall be well again."
*(See Mt. 9:18–26)*


*Cure of the Blind Man at Bethsaida*
[Jesus] took the blind man by the hand and led him outside the village . . . then he laid his hands on the man's eyes again and he saw clearly. *(See Mk. 8:23–26)*


*The Cure of a Sick Man at the Pool of Bethzatha*
[Jesus said] "Do you want to be well again?" "Sir," replied the sick man, "I have no one to put me into the pool . . ." Jesus said, "Get up, pick up your sleeping mat and walk!" The man was cured at once. *(See Jn. 5:1–18)*

---

# For Further Reflection

*The Cure of a Lame Man (See Ac. 3:1–10)*


*Healing of a Cripple (See Ac. 14:8–10)*
Healing is presently entrusted to the Church.

[John the Baptist's disciples asked] "Are you the one who is to come . . . ?" Jesus answered, "Go back and tell John what you hear and see; the blind see again, and the lame walk, lepers are cleansed, and the deaf hear . . ." (Mt. 11:2–6)

# 39

# BREAD OF LIFE

Bread broken; a cup shared. Signs and symbols of a reality far deeper than anything we can imagine; a reality which touches every part of our being. This is the Eucharist, the Bread of Life, given to all so we might live.

What is the sign meant to convey? What is the symbol saying to us as we share the bread and the wine with one another? We know and believe, of course, that it is the Body and Blood of the Lord. Yet it goes beyond that, because the Body and Blood of the Lord includes everything that is of the Lord. And so, when we share the bread and the wine, we are sharing in the reality of God's creation, his being, his life, his all. We are partaking of that which is all in all, as St. Paul tells us.

How does it come about? For many years theologians have tried to establish the "how." We know, of course, that "how" is not of prime importance. What really matters is the fact that this sign and symbol show us the basic reality and nature of God: that he is the one who willingly offers himself in death; that he is the one who willingly accepts powerlessness and simplicity to express his majesty and greatness; that he is the one who accepts brokenness to express wholeness; that he is the one who is food and drink for all who are hungry and thirsty.

Yes, the Eucharist can mean many things, and does mean many things. As a sign and symbol it extends beneath our sensibilities to touch that part of our being which knows no words or language, except the words and language of love.

## Scripture Verses

[Jesus said], . . . give them something to eat yourselves . . .
And breaking the loaves he handed them to his disciples who
gave them to the crowds. They all ate as much as they wanted.
(Mt. 14:16–20)

When the coating of dew lifted, there on the surface of the
desert was a thing delicate, powdery, as fine as hoarfrost on the
ground. When they saw this, the sons of Israel said to one
another, "What is that?" not knowing what it was. "That," said
Moses to them, "is the bread Yahweh gives you to eat."
(Ex. 16:14–15)

I am the bread of life.
He who comes to me will never be hungry;
he who believes in me will never thirst. (Jn. 6:35)

Then he took some bread, and when he had given thanks,
broke it and gave it to them, saying, "This is my body which
will be given for you; do this as a memorial of me." He did the
same with the cup after supper, and said, "This cup is the new
covenant in my blood which will be poured out for you!"
(Lk. 22:19–20)

I tell you most solemnly,
if you do not eat the flesh of the Son of Man
and drink his blood
you will not have life in you.
Anyone who does eat my flesh and drink my blood
has eternal life
and I shall raise him up on the last day. (Jn. 6:53–54)


My flesh is real food
and my blood is real drink.
He who eats my flesh and drinks my blood
lives in me
and I live in him . . .
anyone who eats this bread will live for ever. (Jn. 6:55–58)


Why spend money on what is not bread. (*See* Is. 55:1–3)

―――――❧―――――

## *For Further Reflection*

For the bread of God
is that which comes down from heaven
and gives life to the world. (Jn. 6:33)


I am the bread of life.
Your fathers ate the manna in the desert
and they are dead;
but this is the bread that comes down from heaven,
so that a man may eat it and not die. (Jn. 6:48–50)

I am the living bread which has come down from heaven.
Anyone who eats this bread will live for ever;
and the bread I shall give
is my flesh, for the life of the world. (Jn. 6:51)

# 40

# FREE AT LAST

Over the years we have fought for freedom in several wars of devastating magnitude. In the name of freedom, cities have been leveled, people have been maimed or killed, many have been left starving and homeless. Yet, despite the wars, despite the expense of money, resources, and lives, despite the tears and the sweat and the pain, freedom does not yet exist. Though armies have been assembled, programs initiated, and promises made by political leaders everywhere, freedom continues to elude us.

Perhaps you think yourself free already, living in a country with world status and enviable bounty. Perhaps you think yourself free, distant as you are from countries where oppression runs rampant, and hunger stalks the night. Yet, the fact remains: Freedom, real freedom, eludes us.

Jesus alone is the one who sets us free. He alone is the one who shows us the meaning of freedom, and gives us the way to abide in that freedom. In his death and resurrection, he reveals to us that freedom does not mean license, but privilege; it does not mean free to do what we want, but free to be who we are. Again and again the Lord shows to us that freedom means sonship and daughtership; it means living in the arms of a loving Father; it means accepting our real identity as children of God; it means life here and now in the presence of the Risen Lord.

On the cross Jesus showed us that the freedom won is freedom from fear, freedom from anxiety, freedom from the lies of the Evil One. It is a freedom that offers us the infinite possibilities of God himself: the possibility of love, forgiveness, healing, and joy. This is the freedom given us by Jesus. Do we not say during the Eucharistic Acclamation: "Lord, by your cross and resurrection you have set us free"?

It is real; it is complete; it is tangible; it is gift given by him who gives all. In our prayer let us ask the Lord to show us how his freedom might be integrated into our life. Let us also remember that his freedom is there whether or not we feel it. That it is a reality which does not depend on our "feelings," but on the fact of Jesus's death and resurrection.

## Scripture Verses

The Spirit of Yahweh has been given to me,
for Yahweh has anointed me.
He has sent me to bring good news to the poor,
to bind up hearts that are broken;
to proclaim liberty to captives;
freedom to those in prison. (Is. 61:1)

Before the world was made, he chose us, chose us in Christ . . . through Jesus Christ . . . in whom, through his blood, we gain our freedom, the forgiveness of our sins. (Ep. 1:4–7)

You are slaves of no one except God, so behave like free men, and never use your freedom as an excuse for wickedness. (1 Pt. 2:16)

If what was so temporary [Mosaic Law] had any splendor,
there must be much more in what is going to last for ever . . .
Having this hope we can be quite confident; . . . where the
Spirit of the Lord is, there is freedom. (2 Co. 3:11–17)

If you make my word your home
you will indeed be my disciples,
you will learn the truth
and the truth will make you free . . .
So if the Son makes you free,
you will be free indeed. (Jn. 8:31–36)

He has taken us out of the power of darkness and created a
place for us in the kingdom of the son that he loves, and in him,
we gain our freedom, the forgiveness of our sins. (Col. 1:13–14)

The law of the spirit of life in Christ Jesus has set you free from
the law of sin and death. (Rm. 8:2)

—————◆—————

## For Further Reflection

Yahweh has ransomed Jacob,
rescued him from a hand stronger than his own. (Jr. 31:11)

Thus he shows mercy to our ancestors,
and he remembers his holy covenant . . .
that he would grant us, free from fear,

to be delivered from the hands of our enemies,
to serve him in holiness and virtue
in his presence, all our days. (Lk. 1:72–75)


Christ liberates us from slavery to the Law. (Ga. 3:10–13)

# 41

# LIVING IN THE SPIRIT

Living in the Spirit involves a marvelous blending of divine grace and human work—grace because the Lord acts within us; work because our own efforts and decisions are needed as we move toward the good in conjunction with Christ's teachings. To think it is an easy task is foolish. It is probably the hardest we will ever attempt, since it goes against the very grain of society which does not accept the Lord's way as the way of life.

Perhaps you have often thought that living in the Spirit was such a burden and effort that it was not worth beginning at all. Looking around we see people "doing fine" who are not seemingly following the Lord's precepts. They appear to be joyful and happy, helpful and loving, concerned with others, true humanitarians. This, however, is not living in the Spirit.

Though it seems that living in the Spirit involves rules and regulations, do's and don't's, it really is not so. To approach the scriptures with that mind-set would be to miss the point. The directions that the scripture authors give us are meant to be signs of a person who is living in the Spirit. It is not the action that makes it so, but the Spirit who makes the actions possible. For example, a person who is "in the Lord" would necessarily be growing in humility and love and service. If this growth process is not taking place, it would indicate that the Spirit is not being allowed to transform the individual. If the process is taking place, if a person is growing in these ways, then we can assume that God has his hand on that person.

There are many people whom the Lord is touching with his Spirit. We have met them, churched and unchurched alike. They are showing the signs of living in the Spirit, the signs mentioned especially by St. Paul. Let us not judge how well they are doing, but simply respond with praise when we see God is working in the lives of others.

## Scripture Verses

*General Rules of Christian Behavior: Life in the Spirit*
Be clothed in sincere compassion . . . bear with one another . . . forgive each other . . . put on love . . . And may the peace of Christ reign in your hearts. *(See* Col. 3:5–17)

So be very careful about the sort of lives you lead . . . this may be a wicked age, but your lives should redeem it . . . be filled with the Spirit . . . and go on singing and chanting to the Lord in your hearts . . . giving thanks to God.
(Ep. 5:15–21)

There must be no more lies . . . never let the sun set on your anger . . . Guard against foul talk . . . never have grudges against others . . . Be friends with one another. (Ep. 4:25–32)

You must live your whole life according to the Christ you have received—Jesus the Lord; you must be rooted in him and built on him and held firm by the faith you have been taught, and full of thanksgiving. (Col. 2:6–7)

We urge you . . . to make more and more progress in the kind of life you are meant to live: the life that God wants, . . .

What God wants is for you all to be holy . . . make a point of living quietly. (1 Th. 4:1–12)

Do not model yourselves on the behavior of the world around you, but let your behavior change, modeled by your new mind. (Rm. 12:2)

What the Spirit brings is very different: love, joy, peace, patience, kindness, goodness, trustfulness, gentleness and self-control . . . Since the Spirit is our life, let us be directed by the Spirit. (Ga. 5:22–25)

<hr>

## *For Further Reflection*

Happy the man
who never follows the advice of the wicked,
or loiters on the way that sinners take,
or sits about with scoffers,
but finds his pleasure in the Law of Yahweh. (Ps. 1:1–2)

Bless those who persecute you . . . Treat everyone with equal kindness . . . Never try to get revenge . . . Resist evil and conquer it with good. (Rm. 12:14–21)

Do not let your love be a pretense, . . . Work for the Lord with untiring effort . . . and keep on praying. (Rm. 12:9–12)

# 42

# GOD SPEAKS IN THE DESERT

The ways of the Lord are strange indeed. Who would think that in the desert he would offer us his greatest gifts? Who would think that in the dryness and the barrenness of the desert he could speak his word clearly to a heart willing to listen? Yet this is precisely the case. It has been so throughout the history of salvation. The desert, seen as a wasteland by society, is seen as a place of growth and life by believers.

It is in the desert that we are most dependent upon God. Separated from all life supports, we are moved to place our trust in him; distant from the luxuries which we take for granted, we are now able to come to him with empty hands and heart so he might fill us with his Spirit.

Traditionally there have always been men and women who fled to the desert in order to hear the Lord clearly. They remain a sign and an encouragement to us: a sign of total surrender and dependence on God; an encouragement that it can indeed happen, we can trust in his providence and love.

Each of us needs a desert place. It need not be some distant country or isolated hermitage. It could be the kitchen table shorn of plates and debris, and decorated, for the moment, with only a Bible. It could be a tiny area of a room, or a special time of day; a chair, a church, a favorite lake, etc. Where our desert is, or how it looks, is inconsequential. What matters is that we go there and listen to him speak.

## Scripture Verses

Filled with the Holy Spirit, Jesus left the Jordan and was led by the Spirit through the wilderness, being tempted there by the devil for forty days. *(See* Lk. 4:1–13)

I am the true vine,
and my Father is the vinedresser . . .
every branch that does not bear fruit he prunes
to make it bear even more. (Jn. 15:1–2)

I am going to lure her
and lead her out into the wilderness
and speak to her heart . . .
There she will respond to me as she did when she was
    young . . .
I will betroth you to myself forever . . .
with tenderness and love; . . .
and you will come to know Yahweh. (Ho. 2:16–22)

Let the wilderness and the dry lands exult,
let the wasteland rejoice and bloom . . .
they shall see the glory of Yahweh . . .
Strengthen all weary hands,
steady all trembling knees
and say to all faint hearts,
"Courage! Do not be afraid,
"Look, your God is coming . . ." (Is. 35:1–4)

In the desert I will plant juniper, . . .
so that men may see and know,
may all observe and understand
that the hand of Yahweh has done this. (Is. 41:19–20)


The poor and needy ask for water, and there is none,
their tongue is parched with thirst.
I, Yahweh, will answer them,
I, the God of Israel, will not abandon them. (Is. 41:17)


The apostles rejoined Jesus and told him all they had done and taught. Then he said to them, "You must come away to some lonely place all by yourselves and rest for a while." (Mk. 6:30–31)

---

## For Further Reflection

Now I am making the whole of creation new . . . I am the Alpha and the Omega, the Beginning and the End. (Rv. 21:5–6)


The woman escaped into the desert, where God had made a place of safety ready, for her to be looked after. (Rv. 12:6)


Beside me your rod and your staff
are there, to hearten me. (Ps. 23:4)

# 43

# ROOTED IN LOVE

To be rooted in love is to be rooted in life. It is to be rooted in God himself, for, as St. John tells us, "God is love." Life and love are synonymous in this context because everything springs from God, who is love. To be alive, therefore, means that we are alive in Jesus, the Crucified One raised from the dead. To be rooted in love means the same, namely, to be in the Crucified One raised from the dead.

This takes place as we allow the power of the Holy Spirit to be the binding force that joins us to the Lord and to one another. Knit together as one with Christ, and with each other, we are now able to "breathe" together; we are able to move as one, for in Christ we are one. Therefore, one's life necessarily affects another's because in Christ crucified all are one.

Perhaps the greatest and most tangible sign of the Lord's power in our midst is the practical signs of love we are allowed to share with one another: a kiss, a word of thanks or encouragement, a listening ear, an attentive glance. This is the love which can turn the world upside down because things are finally seen right side up; a love which reaches out to others because Jesus's reach has already been felt; a love that allows us to know in the depths of our being the utter fullness of God.

## Scripture Verses

The greatest of these is love. *(See* 1 Co. 13)

[May Christ] live in your hearts . . . and then, planted in love and built on love, you will with all the saints have strength to grasp the breadth and the length, the height and the depth; until . . . you are filled with the utter fullness of God. (Ep. 3:17–19)

If we live by the truth and in love, we shall grow in all ways into Christ, who is the head by whom the whole body is fitted and joined together, every joint adding its own strength, for each separate part to work according to its function. So the body grows until it has built itself up, in love. (Ep. 4:15–16)

It is love that helps us grow in unity. (1 Co. 8:1–3)

Being rooted in love is shown by our willingness to receive the inner. (2 Co. 2:5–11)

Rooted in love we are free from fear. (1 Jn. 4:17–18)

The love of God has been poured into our hearts by the Holy Spirit which has been given us. (Rm. 5:5)

---

## For Further Reflection

Above all, never let your love for each other grow insincere, since love covers over many a sin. (1 Pt. 4:8)

Be an example to all the believers . . . in your love, your faith, and your purity. (1 Tm. 4:12)

Be clothed in sincere compassion, in kindness and humility, gentleness and patience . . . Over all these clothes, to keep them together and complete them, put on love. (Col. 3:12–14)

# 44

# FRUIT THAT LASTS

Christianity is not a flash in the pan. Those who intend to remain united to the Lord Jesus must remain steady for the long run, the entire race, if the victory is to be permanently integrated into their life. This is especially true as the transforming power of the Spirit changes us bit by bit in a steady, gradual, and permanent way.

Throughout this process we need to remain on our guard, especially during the initial stages of our growth in the Lord. Too often the "changes" in our life come so quickly they barely have time to take root. In our enthusiasm, we tend to bite off more than we can manage, thereby bringing about a type of spiritual indigestion, such as, a life-style filled with spiritual superficialities, but not integrated with our humanity.

As we grow in the Lord, therefore, we are called to bear fruit that lasts; we are called to remain part of the vine which gives us strength, and willing participants in the pruning process which brings about growth. In doing this we will surely bear the fruit that lasts since we will be bearing the fruit which stems from the Tree of Life itself.

## Scripture Verses

Serve one another, rather in works of love . . . If you go on snapping at each other and tearing each other to pieces, you had better watch or you will destroy the whole community. (Ga. 5:13–15)

Fasten your attention on holiness, faith, love and peace, in union with all those who call on the Lord with pure minds. *(See* 2 Tm. 2:22–26)

A sound tree produces good fruit . . . you will be able to tell them by their fruits. *(See* Mt. 7:15–20)

As a branch cannot bear fruit all by itself,
but must remain part of the vine,
neither can you unless you remain in me. (Jn. 15:4–8)

Where a man sows, there he reaps: if he sows in the field of the Spirit he will get from it a harvest of eternal life. (Ga. 6:7–8)

From the fruits of virtue grows a tree of life. (Pr. 11:30)

What the Spirit brings is very different: love, joy, peace, patience, kindness, goodness, trustfulness, gentleness and self-control. (Ga. 5:22–23)

* * *

## For Further Reflection

A good man draws what is good from the store of goodness in his heart; a bad man draws what is bad from the store of badness. *(See* Lk. 6:43–45)

The kingdom of God does not mean eating or drinking this or that, it means righteousness and peace and joy brought by the Holy Spirit. If you serve Christ in this way you will please God and be respected by men. (Rm. 14:17–18)

Along the river, on either bank, will grow every kind of fruit tree with leaves that never wither and fruit that never fails; they will bear new fruit every month, because this water comes from the sanctuary. *(See* Ez. 47:1–12)

# 45

# SEEK THE LORD

To seek implies a journey, a looking and searching, a listening. It is a reorientation of priorities, placing that which is sought on the top of the list. It means a life-style change involving the use of time, money, talents, etc. Many people, for example, seek higher positions at work, different material benefits such as houses, cars, and boats; others seek a particular relationship or friendship which may lead to lifelong commitments. It all requires a reordering of time, and a deliberate way of proceeding.

Seeking also implies that we have not yet found that which we are seeking. The person striving for a better position at work has not yet received it; the individual saving for a second car has not yet acquired it; the person trying to strike up a friendship with another has not yet succeeded.

In all of these examples, success will come about to the degree that the individual gives it a priority in his/her life. If the attempt is halfhearted, the result will be negligible. If the attempt is focused and deliberate, the result will probably be positive.

Such is the case when we seek the Lord. A halfhearted attempt will bring about an incomplete result; an enthusiastic, focused attempt, however, will undoubtedly bring us to the God whom we seek. During prayer, keep in your heart the beautiful fact that God seeks us also. He does this in Jesus, his Son, through the abiding presence of the Spirit. As we seek him, therefore, he is already seeking us, showing us the way to find him. Who was more focused or deliberate, wholehearted or untiring than Jesus as he sought us even unto death on the cross? Through that example, he shows us the way to seek the Father namely, by imitating the way he has chosen to seek us.

## Scripture Verses

When you seek me you shall find me, when you seek me with all
your heart; I will let you find me. (Jr. 29:13–14)


Seek Yahweh while he is still to be found,
call to him while he is still near. *(See* Is. 55:6–9)


If you seek him with all your heart and with all your soul, you
shall find him. In your distress, all that I have said will overtake
you, but at the end of days you will return to Yahweh your God
and listen to his voice. (Dt. 4:29–30)


All the runners at the stadium are trying to win, but only one
of them gets the prize . . . That is how I run, intent on win-
ning. (1 Co. 9:24–26)


For Yahweh says this to the House of Israel.
Seek me and you shall live . . .
Do not seek Bethel, . . .
do not journey to Beersheba, . . .
Seek Yahweh and you shall live. (Am. 5:4–6)

Seek Yahweh and his strength,
seek his face untiringly;
remember the marvels he has done,
his wonders, the judgments from his mouth. (Ps. 105:4–5)


Set your hearts on his kingdom first, and on his righteousness.
(Mt. 6:33)

---

## For Further Reflection

We beg you . . . not to neglect the grace of God that you have
received. For he says: At the favorable time I have listened to
you; on the day of salvation I came to your help. Well, now is
the favorable time; this is the day of salvation. (2 Co. 6:1–2)


The Magi sought the Lord by following a star. (Mt. 2:1–12)


We continually seek God in prayer. (Ps. 27:8)

# 46

# JESUS: A SELF-PORTRAIT

When praying the Beatitudes, we often approach them as ideals toward which we must strive. In reality, however, they are meant to reveal the self-identity of Jesus, and, by association, they also reveal the identity of any individual who follows the Lord, since he/she will necessarily be one with Christ. The Beatitudes, therefore, are not presented as rules and regulations which must be followed if we are to be saved, but as the revelation of Jesus's self-identity, and our self-identity as believers.

Imagine yourself on the Mount as Jesus begins to preach. Slowly and deliberately he presents what seems to be an impossible ideal. Upon examining his life, however, it can be seen that Jesus is merely explaining to the people who he is as Child of God: He is the one poor in spirit; the one who mourns for others; the one persecuted; the one who is singlehearted; the one who hungers for justice, etc. This is Jesus's many-faceted identity, all stemming, of course, from the reality of his Sonship which he freely accepts from the Father.

See in the Beatitudes, therefore, a self-portrait of Jesus. And see in Jesus a possible portrait of yourself.

# Scripture Verses

The Beatitudes. (Mt. 5:3–12)

I am the good shepherd:
the good shepherd is one who lays down his life for his
     sheep.
I know my own
and my own know me. (Jn. 10:11–14)

I am the light of the world;
anyone who follows me will not be walking in the dark;
he will have the light of life. (Jn. 8:12)

I am the Way, the Truth, and the Life.
No one can come to the Father except through me. (Jn. 14:6)

I am the bread of life.
He who comes to me will never be hungry;
he who believes in me will never thirst. (Jn. 6:35–40)

I am the resurrection.
If anyone believes in me, even though he dies he will live,
and whoever lives and believes in me
will never die. *(See* Jn. 11:1–44)

I am the Living One, I was dead and now I am to live for ever
and ever. (Rv. 1:17–18)

---

## *For Further Reflection*

I am the gate of the sheepfold.
All others who have come
are thieves and brigands, . . .
I am the gate.
Anyone who enters through me will be safe. (Jn. 10:7–9)

I am the true vine
and my Father is the vinedresser . . .
Make your home in me as I make mine in you . . .
I am the vine
you are the branches. (Jn. 15:1–5)

The high priest put a second question to him, "Are you the
Christ," he said, "the Son of the Blessed One?" "I am," said
Jesus. (Mk. 14:61–62)

# 47

# LIVING IN FAITH

To live in faith is to live in the Kingdom of God. It is to accept as reality that which the Lord Jesus has shown us, through his death and resurrection, as real. This reality involves the Father's forgiveness, the sending of the Spirit, and the gift of sonship/daughtership offered to those who believe.

This Kingdom, in which only those in faith can live, remains unseen to unbelievers, yet tangibly present to men and women of faith. Look, for example, at the lives of the saints. They are believers who live in faith, thereby gaining access to the Kingdom. Though the reality of this Kingdom remains "unseen" to many, it remains their life's bread nonetheless. St. Francis of Assisi is a good example. His life of faith enabled him to accept the Kingdom as his only reality. Such rootedness in God enabled him to talk to animals, heal people, remain filled with joy and peace despite physical suffering and pain. How could this be, we might ask? Simply put, it is faith—a living in faith which gave him access to the deepest reality, God himself.

Living in faith, therefore, goes beyond doctrines and dogmas; it goes beyond ritual and religious formulations. It involves accepting the Kingdom of God as a Kingdom present to us now. Present to us so we might live now in Jesus, with the Father, embraced by the Spirit.

## Scripture Verses

Only faith can guarantee the blessings we hope for, or prove the existence of the realities that at present remain unseen. (Heb. 11:1)

You must live your whole life according to the Christ you have received—Jesus the Lord; you must be rooted in him and built on him and held firm by the faith you have been taught, and full of thanksgiving. (Col. 2:6–7)

The language of the cross may be illogical to those who are not on the way to salvation, but those of us who are on the way see it as God's power to save . . . because God wanted to save those who have faith through the foolishness of the message we preach. (1 Co. 1:18–21)

Faith without good deeds is useless. (Jm. 2:20)

Persevere and stand firm on the solid base of the faith, never letting yourself drift away from the hope promised by the Good News. (Col. 1:23)

Take the case . . . of someone who has never done a single good act but claims that he has faith. Will that faith save him? . . . if good works do not go with it, it is quite dead. (Jm. 2:14–17)

Were your faith the size of a mustard seed you could say to this mulberry tree, "Be uprooted and planted in the sea," and it would obey you. (Lk. 17:6)

---

## For Further Reflection

Faith comes from what is preached, and what is preached comes from the word of Christ. (Rm. 10:17)

A body dies when it is separated from the spirit, and in the same way faith is dead if it is separated from good deeds. (Jm. 2:26)

Some people have put conscience aside and wrecked their faith in consequence. (1 Tm. 1:19)

# 48

# GIVE THANKS TO THE LORD

Prayers of thankfulness need not be formal, lengthy, or extended in time. In fact, they are best expressed in short phrases repeated over and over in our heart. One might say they are inner attitudes spoken by the heart, not the mind or the lips.

Rather than get bogged down with a formalized period of thanks during our prayer period, therefore, it might be helpful to attempt shorter periods of thanks throughout the day. For example, try repeating the phrase, "Thank you, Lord, for . . ." as often as you can during the day. You will find it opens your heart to a spirit of thanks that eventually becomes constant, while at the same time it transcends consciousness.

In your prayer, do not hesitate to thank the Lord for all that he gives. This is often difficult since we are not always willing to receive some of the "gifts" which make little sense to us. Yet all is gift from God, and all his gifts deserve a prayer of thanks. In addition, try to be sensitive to the movement of the Spirit who will lead you in this type of prayer. You might find, for example, that your mind is suddenly "wandering" in a wordless type of prayer, or an inner, affective prayer which fills you with consolation. Use this as an indication that the Lord wants you to thank him for his presence, his love, his gifts. Do not let these moments pass by unacknowledged, since you would be ignoring a time of grace.

# Scripture Verses

I thank you, Yahweh, with all my heart,
because you have heard what I said . . .
I give thanks to your name for your love and faithfulness.
(Ps. 138:1–2)

[The leper] finding himself cured . . . threw himself at the feet
of Jesus and thanked him. *(See* Lk. 17:11–19)

For all things give thanks to God, because this is what God
expects you to do in Christ Jesus. (1 Th. 5:18)

I thank you, Yahweh, with all my heart;
I recite your marvels one by one,
I rejoice and exult in you,
I sing praise to your name, Most High. (Ps. 9:1–2)

Let us thank God for giving us the victory through our Lord
Jesus Christ. (1 Co. 15:57)

Since grace is given so fully, the Christian is called to thank
God in every situation. (1 Co. 1:4–9)

*Litany of Thanksgiving*
Give thanks to Yahweh, for he is good. *(See* Ps. 136)

---

## *For Further Reflection*

Blessed be God the Father of our Lord Jesus Christ, who has blessed us with all the spiritual blessings of heaven in Christ. *(See* Ep. 1:3–10)

Blessed be you, Yahweh our God,
from everlasting to everlasting . . .
you made the heavens . . . with all their array . . .
To all these you give life. (Ne. 9:5–6)

*Hymn of Thanksgiving*
I give thanks to your name for your love and faithfulness.
     *(See* Ps. 138)

# 49

# THE LORD IS RISEN—REJOICE!

His body could not contain all the Father desired to give. So pleased was the Father with the obedience of Jesus, his Son, that the Spirit, sent to embrace Jesus within the tomb, penetrated his human body with everything that was the Father's. Yet Jesus's weak, broken humanity could not contain all that the Father offered, and so, in the words of St. Paul, Jesus received a new body, a spiritual body, which could contain the fullness of God in his human flesh raised from the dead.

The how of it all is not important. What is essential, however, is the fact of resurrection. Jesus, the Son of God, united to us in our humanity, was raised from the dead so that we too might be raised up with him.

Since we were unable to respond completely to the Father on our own, Jesus, through his obedience, responded for us so that in him we might reap the benefits of his perfect response. This is why Jesus's resurrection is the core reality of our faith. Without it we would still be unable to accept all the gifts that the Father offers us, particularly his gift of sonship/daughtership. Without Jesus's resurrection, we would remain stymied by our human frailty and sinfulness, by our limitations and finitude. Yet, Jesus, God-man, perfectly joining in his flesh the Divine who is love and the human who is recipient of love, unilaterally makes it possible for us to accept all that the Father offers. And so, rejoice, for the Lord is risen. Alleluia.

## Scripture Verses

The angel spoke; and he said to the women, "There is no need for you to be afraid. I know you are looking for Jesus, who was crucified. He is not here, for he has risen, as he said he would." *(See* Mt. 28:1–10)

[Simon Peter] went right into the tomb, saw the linen cloths on the ground, and also the cloth that had been over his head; . . . he saw and he believed. *(See* Jn. 20:1–10)

As Christ was raised from the dead by the Father's glory, we too might live a new life . . . Christ, as we know, having been raised from the dead will never die again. Death has no power over him any more. (Rm. 6:4–10)

But Christ has in fact been raised from the dead . . . Death came through one man and in the same way the resurrection of the dead has come through one man . . . so all men will be brought to life in Christ. (1 Co. 15:20–22)

Now while he was with them at table, he took the bread and said the blessing; then he broke it and handed it to them. And their eyes were opened and they recognized him. *(See* Lk. 24:13–35)

He himself stood among them and said to them, "Peace be with you!" . . . "Look at my hands and my feet; yes, it is I indeed. Touch me and see for yourselves . . ." *(See* Lk. 24:36–43)

Then he spoke to Thomas, "Put your finger here; look, here are my hands. Give me your hand; put it into my side. Doubt no longer but believe." . . .
"You believe because you can see me.
Happy are those who have not seen and yet believe."
(Jn. 20:27–29)

---

## For Further Reflection

What he [David the prophet] foresaw and spoke about was the resurrection of Christ: . . . God raised this man Jesus to life, and all of us are witnesses to that. (Ac. 2:31)

May the God of our Lord Jesus Christ . . . bring you to full knowledge . . . May he enlighten the eyes of your mind so you can see . . . how infinitely great is the power that he has exercised for us believers. This you can tell from the strength of his power at work in Christ, when he used it to raise him from the dead. (Ep. 1:17–20)

The appearance to Mary Magdalen. (Jn. 20:11–18)

# 50

# DEATH, WHERE IS YOUR VICTORY?

Perhaps you have turned to this section because someone you love has died. Your grief is undoubtedly overwhelming. Fear, frustration, anger, helplessness are some of the many feelings that are probably wracking your entire being. On top of that, you might also be wondering why your faith is not protecting you from these feelings. The entire world looks dark.

The words of scripture presented here are most helpful when we are asked to meditate on the reality of death. They do not try to answer the question "Why?" but simply state the fact of Jesus's resurrection. They do not try to "make it all better," but simply remind us of Jesus's victory over death.

Do not, therefore, believe what you see when confronted with the mystery of death. For what you see is a humiliation and an abomination; you see life supposedly ended and love snatched away. Rather, see what you believe. And what we believe is the victory of the Lord, the resurrection of the dead, the enduring love of the Father who never forces evil upon us. Yes, see what you believe, that he who is risen calls us always to life, and the death we see is really no-thing for us to fear.

## Scripture Verses

Death was not God's doing,
he takes no pleasure in the extinction of the living.
To be—for this he created all; . . .

and Hades holds no power on earth;
for virtue is undying. (Ws. 1:13–15)


The Lord Yahweh says this: I am now going to open your
graves; I mean to raise you from your graves, my people, . . .
and you will know that I am Yahweh, when I open your graves
and raise you from your graves, my people. And I shall put my
spirit in you, and you will live. (Ez. 37:12–14)


Now if Christ raised from the dead is what has been
preached, how can some of you be saying that there is no resurrection of the dead? . . . For if the dead are not raised, Christ
has not been raised . . .
But Christ has in fact been raised from the dead.
(1 Co. 15:12–20)


We believe that Jesus died and rose again, and that it will be the
same for those who have died in Jesus: God will bring them
with him. (1 Th. 4:14)


On this mountain he will remove
the mourning veil covering all peoples,
and the shroud enwrapping all nations,
he will destroy Death for ever. (Is. 25:7–8)


After that [the resurrection in Christ] will come the end, when
he [Jesus] hands over the kingdom to God the Father, . . .
having done away with every sovereignty, authority and power

. . . and the last of the enemies to be destroyed is death.
(1 Co. 15:24–26)

When this perishable nature has put on imperishability, . . .
then the words of scripture will come true: Death is swallowed
up in victory. Death, where is your victory? Death, where is
your sting? (1 Co. 15:54–57)

---

## For Further Reflection

This I know: that My Avenger lives,
and he, the Last, will take his stand on earth.
After my awakening he will set me close to him,
and from my flesh I shall look on God. (Jb. 29:25–27)

[Jesus] abolished death, and he has proclaimed life and immor-
tality through the Good News. (2 Tm. 1:10)

And we so have no eyes for things that are visible, but only for
things that are invisible; for visible things last only for a time,
and the invisible things are eternal.

For we know that when the tent that we live in on earth is
folded up, there is a house built by God for us, an everlasting
home not made by human hands, in the heavens.
(2 Co. 4:18–5:1)

# 51

# BE PREPARED AND WAIT FOR THE LORD

It never ceases to amaze me how God uses everyday, normal experiences to teach us something about his relationship to us, and our relationship to him. It was precisely as I was preparing this section of the book when I took a break for dinner. Being alone, I went to a neighborhood restaurant that I frequent. On that particular day, I was struck by the waiter who served the table. He was an amazing young man, attentive but not overbearing, present yet not in the way, friendly and cheerful but not superficial. He anticipated my needs, and was willing to move things along at the rate I desired. In short, he was an excellent waiter.

When I returned to work, the insight came suddenly. We Christians are called to be "waiters": called to prepare for the Lord's return by "waiting" patiently, and by "waiting" on others. This is precisely the sign which people need if they are to see the reality of Jesus in their midst. They need to see Christians living their life as "waiters": waiters for the Lord, and waiters, that is, servants, for their neighbors. In doing so we would be ordering our lives according to the promises of Jesus who tells us to prepare in every way for his return. What better way to prepare than to wait on our neighbors as we joyfully wait for his coming in glory.

Like the waiter in that restaurant, therefore, we too are called to anticipate the needs of our neighbors, to be cheerful, friendly, and attentive to their well-being. Then we will be Jesus for them; then we will be prepared to meet the Lord when he comes.

## Scripture Verses

Be calm but vigilant, because your enemy the devil is prowling around like a roaring lion, looking for someone to eat. Stand up to him, strong in faith. (1 Pt. 5:8–9)

Besides, you know "the time" has come: you must wake up now: our salvation is even nearer than it was when we were converted. The night is almost over, it will be daylight soon— let us give up all things we prefer to do under cover of dark; let us arm ourselves and appear in the light. (Rm. 13:11–12)

You know that the day of the Lord is going to come like a thief in the night . . . and there will be no way for anybody to evade it . . . stay wide awake and sober . . . give encouragement to each other, and keep strengthening one another as you already do. (1 Th. 5:1–11)

[When the Lord comes] He will light up all that is hidden in the dark and reveal the secret intentions of men's hearts. Then will be the time for each one to have whatever praise he deserves, from God. (1 Co. 4:5)

So stay awake, because you do not know the day when your master is coming. You may be quite sure of this that if the householder had known at what time of the night the burglar would come, he would have stayed awake and not have allowed anyone to break through the wall of his house. Therefore, you too must stand ready because the Son of Man is coming at an hour you do not expect. (Mt. 24:42–44)

Now be patient, brothers, until the Lord's coming. Think of a farmer: how patiently he waits for the precious fruit of the ground until it has the autumn rains and the spring rains! You too have to be patient; do not lose heart, because the Lord's coming will be soon. (Jm. 5:7–8)

But there is one thing, my friends, that you must never forget: that with the Lord, "a day" can mean a thousand years and a thousand years is like a day. The Lord is not being slow in carrying out his promises . . . he is being patient with you all. (2 Pt. 3:8–9)

## For Further Reflection

I want you to be happy, always happy in the Lord; . . . let your tolerance be evident to everyone: the Lord is very near. There is no need to worry . . . fill your minds with everything that is true . . . noble, . . . good and pure. (Ph. 4:4–8)

For us, our homeland is in heaven, and from heaven comes the Savior we are waiting for, the Lord Jesus Christ, and he will transfigure these wretched bodies of ours into copies of his glorious body. (Ph. 3:20–21)

The witness to Christ has indeed been strong among you so that you will not be without any of the gifts of the Spirit while you are waiting for our Lord Jesus Christ to be revealed; and he will keep you steady and without blame until the last day, the day of our Lord Jesus Christ, because God by calling you has joined you to his Son, Jesus Christ; and God is faithful. (1 Co. 1:6–9)

# 52

# THY KINGDOM COME

The Lord's Prayer states it as a promise and a hope: "Thy Kingdom come." Perhaps it has become a rote prayer, an unreflective utterance carrying little meaning or hope. Yet, the coming of God's Kingdom is the final embrace of love which the Father desires to give us. It is the final, Divine utterance which will echo throughout eternity proving his desire to unite us to himself in his Son, Jesus.

The early Church Fathers saw in the promised Kingdom the coming of the Holy Spirit. Here was the Kingdom of the Father and the Son, tangibly present to us. Here, in the eternal kiss of God, we would be caught up in ecstasy with the Creator and Lord of all. In the binding love of Father and Son we would live as they: one, united, distinct, divine, eternal. It would all take place in the Kingdom, that is, in the Spirit.

At first glance, the scriptures might seem to convey another experience, namely, fear rather than love. In reality, however, God's Word is simply trying to show us how we can be prepared to receive the life of the Kingdom, the life of the Spirit, completely. We are called to be emptied, purified, shorn of all attachments so we can totally accept the fullness of life that the Kingdom offers.

This fullness is God himself communicating his trinitarian reality to us through the unifying power of his Spirit. For it is in the Spirit, in the Kingdom, that the Father and the Son live for and in and with one another. Therefore, we can experience the same Kingdom living as we allow the Spirit of the Father and the Son to embrace us in the same way he embraces them.

"Thy Kingdom come," therefore, is not a prayer for a material kingdom. It is not a prayer for a place, a new institution, a country, or a future event. It is a prayer for the Spirit of God to come and let the reality of God be our reality also.

## Scripture Verses

In the days to come
the mountain of the Temple of Yahweh
shall tower above the mountains
and be lifted higher than the hills.
All the nations will stream to it,
peoples without number will come to it; and they will say:
"Come, let us go up to the mountain of Yahweh . . .
that he may teach us his ways
so that we may walk in his paths." (Is. 2:2–3)


Jesus replied, "Mine is not a kingdom of this world; . . . Yes, I am a king . . . I came into this world for this: to bear witness to the truth; and all who are on the side of truth listen to my voice. (Jn. 18:36–37)


After that I saw a huge number, impossible to count, of people from every nation . . . They shouted aloud, "Victory to our God, who sits on the throne, and to the Lamb!" And all the angels . . . prostrated themselves before the throne . . . worshiping God. (Rv. 7:9–12)


This is what the kingdom of God is like. A man threw seed on the land. Night and day, while he sleeps, when he is awake, the seed is sprouting and growing; how, he does not know.
(See Mk. 4:26–29)

[The Kingdom] is like a mustard seed which at the time of its sowing in the soil is the smallest of all the seeds on earth; yet once it is sown it grows into the biggest shrub of them all. (Mk. 4:31–32)

Riches are an impediment to a person's entering the kingdom. (Mk. 10:23–27)

Jesus exclaimed, "I bless you, Father, Lord of heaven and of earth, for hiding these things from the learned and the clever and revealing them to mere children." (Mt. 11:25–26)

―――――∞―――――

## For Further Reflection

They will live without fear and no one will disturb them again. *(See* Ez. 34:26–31)

You must not set your hearts on things to eat and things to drink; nor must you worry . . . No, set your hearts on his kingdom. (Lk. 12:22–32)

The kingdom is for all. (Mt. 20:1–15)

# APPENDIX A

## *Spiritual/Psychological Explanation of the Journey*

Since God has spoken through the image of the journey, indeed, since he has allowed it to be his own pattern of self-revelation, we would do well to understand the personal journey-image planted within our hearts. We are supported in this quest through the writings of the saints, many of whom have written specifically of the soul's journey to God. In studying the works of these sojourners, we notice a pattern emerge: similar signs, stages, and experiences seem to fall together in related categories. What follows is a compilation and synthesis of these ideas. They are offered so you might come to understand the journey-image, and recognize it in your own life. Although not the specific format of any one sojourner, I believe the following synthesis echoes and resounds with the work and experience of those who have journeyed before us.

Before we begin, it must be emphasized that the categories and descriptions presented here are not absolute. It would be incorrect for you to lock yourself into any one description of phase of growth, and say, "That is I." The categories are not as neat and defined as they appear to be. The descriptions that follow are meant to be a teaching and discovery aid, not an ultimate or easy way to find out precisely where you are on the journey.

In the following diagram we have a basic schema for spiritual growth. It is a movement through life's experiences toward our accepting the invitation of union with God. This journey from self to Other, in whom we discover our real identity is one

**DIAGRAM OF SPIRITUAL GROWTH**

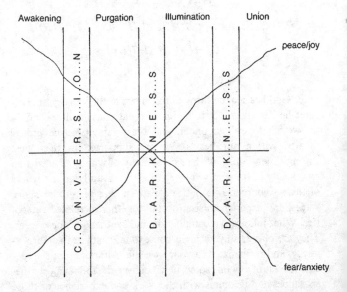

which all people, believers or unbelievers, make. When one studies the history of world religions it becomes clear how universal this schema is. Regardless of religious affiliation, or lack thereof, we are called to make the journey, to travel deep within where the God of Abraham, Isaac, and Jacob dwells through the power of the Holy Spirit.

As a believer in Jesus's salvific message, Christians acknowledge that this universal journey will echo the death/life pattern of the Lord. For both believer and atheist, this pattern is recognizable in creation, as well as in the experience of humankind. As believers, however, our knowledge of and reliance on Jesus's own journey from death to life, help us "find" our way. With this as our focus, we are able to listen to his voice and recognize the signs of his presence as we journey to the Father.

For those not gifted with faith in Jesus's death and resurrection as the journey for all, the path can be wide and winding; signposts and guidelines can be blurred and far apart, making it more difficult to travel. This is why the scripture passage, "Enter through the narrow gate . . ." (Mt. 7:13–14) is a consoling word for those who accept Jesus as the way to the Father.

There is a danger, of course: to look at the above diagram and standardize it for everyone. That is, to insist that my personal journey be identical in all details to another's journey which in turn must be identical in all details to Jesus's journey. Falling into this trap would be unfortunate since no diagram neatly contains or summarizes the unique, individual way God chooses to call us to himself.

The diagram, therefore, is not meant to box God into a neat package, or a particular mode of operation. For example, in studying the diagram it would be incorrect to conclude that each category listed—Awakening, Purgation, Illumination, Union—is a clearly defined stage which a person achieves, passes through, then leaves behind during his/her life. This is simply not the case. In fact, the stages noted in the diagram seem to flow back and forth, one to another, throughout a person's life, so that even in Union a type of purgation continues; even in Purgation the fruit of illumination is often savored.

With this in mind we can now inspect each category mentioned to see how it interrelates with the others. At the same time, several signposts and reference points will be described which might enable you to chart your own journey. Remember, however, that the descriptions offered are not meant to be absolute in their imagery or vocabulary. We are seldom able to chart our personal journey with the precision and exactness longed for. Too much movement is involved: when we think we are at one place, we suddenly find ourselves elsewhere. Regardless of the diagram's limitations, however, we can still discover a rough outline of the path taken as we strive to respond to God's call of Union with him.

## *Awakening/Conversion*

In order to understand this initial stage, imagine a young man very much in love with a girl at his office. She, however, takes little notice of him. Undaunted, the young man strives in every way possible to get her attention: flowers, love letters, telephone calls, a gentle touch, a helping hand, etc. Finally, she takes notice, and begins to respond to his promptings. She is "awakened" to the young man's advances, and responds.

Perhaps what caught her attention was a special note he sent, or an unsolicited gesture of approval and affirmation. Perhaps he said the right word at the right time, or protected her from failing to meet a deadline. The concrete moment or experience which opened her eyes to the young man's advances could have been any one thing at all—or the steady accumulation of many things.

So it is with us and God. He is constantly expressing, in every way possible, his concern, love, and desire for our well-being. Again and again he bombards our senses and faculties with gestures of love, trying to gain our attention. Using every way conceivable—a kiss, an answered prayer, a crisis, a moment of peace, a sunset, a walk on the beach, etc.—he beckons us to acknowledge and accept his advances. Like the young woman who suddenly "notices" the young man, so we, at this initial stage, suddenly notice God. We become aware of his presence, and begin to respond.

It should be noted that this stage requires both an awareness (awakening), and a response (conversion). The process would not be complete, for example, if a person said, "I see God in the sunrise," yet did not respond to that insight in some way. The response (conversion) might be as dramatic as repentance and deep sorrow for sin, or as simple as a decision to return the next day to "see" God in the sunrise again! For the awakening process to be complete, however, a conversion response is necessary, lest the experience remain unintegrated within our inner being.

As you can imagine, such a process can and does occur many times. This is quite similar to our human experience. Take, for example, the young man and woman previously mentioned. Will her response (or even lack of response) curtail the man's continued attempts to advance even closer to her? Of course not. He will continue to "send signals" assuring her, and reminding her of his attentive heart. And she, in turn, by accepting and acknowledging these "signals," will continue to respond anew.

So it is with us and God. Regardless of time spent on the journey, God continually sends us "signals," often called graces, which can awaken us to see, accept, and respond to the infinite depth of his love. Whether or not we respond (convert) completely, partially, or not at all, does not diminish his desire to extend signs of his love and presence to us. Each time we respond, however, the infinite richness and presence of the signs become more apparent to us.

This initial process, therefore, never ceases. It continues throughout our lives as God, pouring his goodness upon us, leads us to acknowledge our need for repentance and conversion (Rm. 2:4). In a sense, we might say that this initial process of awakening continues into eternity since we can never deplete the infinite resource of God's love unfolding before us, beckoning us to an ever deeper response in love.

## *Purgation*

The second stage of our journey can be called Purgation. I use this word with great reluctance, however, since it brings to mind the notion of physical pain and suffering, whereas this part of our journey may not involve "suffering" at all. Often it is filled with consolations and "rewards" which are given to encourage us as we commit ourselves to the Lord.

Basically, then, this is a time when mind and heart are reorganized, having been stung by the Lord's words, "No man can serve two masters." It is a time of reordering values and priorities so we can move toward loving God for his own sake rather than loving God for our own sake, i.e., because he has done something for us.

Perhaps this is where the idea of suffering enters, since any sincere reorganization of life's values requires a stripping, a vulnerability, a painful letting go of the past, as we graft on the new. This might sometimes manifest itself in a dramatic lifestyle change: the drug addict who is "saved"; the atheist who "sees a light" as the doctors pronounce him/her dead, only to witness his/her return to life; the teenager who makes an encounter weekend; the person who receiving the Baptism of the Spirit begins to live in a different way.

The "purgation" witnessed in the cases cited involved a dramatic stripping. In many others, however, the process and challenge to integrate the conversion experience is far more subtle and gradual. Do not, therefore, look only for the dramatic. Look also for the gradual process of being opened and purified; of allowing defense mechanisms to surface and come under con-

trol. Look for a growing self-awareness as false values, seen for
what they are, are gradually relinquished.

The dangers and pitfalls in this stage are legion. Often a person feels he/she has made it and that the process is now over,
the "saving" done: Nothing can now go wrong; it no longer
matters what "sins" I commit. Such an approach would embrace the cheap-grace syndrome which tends to plague movements of enthusiasm: Just say the right words and all is well.

Another danger is to remain fixated at this stage, seeking
only the rewards, that is, salvation, and the experience of feeling
saved, rather than the Reality who offers the grace. This approach prevents our being stripped completely; it keeps us on a
superficial level in our relationship with God, with others, and
with ourselves. Within this mind-set we become convinced that
our actions or our activity produces the desired result—union
with God—rather than seeing how our actions, when purified
properly, really stem from the love of God already present. In
this stage a person does virtuous things; it is the next stage in
which he/she begins to become virtuous.

As in all the stages of our spiritual journey, the purgative
stage does not come to an end. We are constantly being stripped
of our false self, our false identity, our false roles. Even the
"saint" goes through this stage again and again, not because
God wants him/her to "suffer," but because the saint, in uncov-
ering and accepting the true Center, realizes how far he/she
remains from that which is God. For this reason, penance, mortification, fasting, etc., become staples of the journey. We never
outgrow them, but always find in them a source of strength, and
a means of growth. They become, in a sense, the "signals" or
"signposts" that the novice needs in order to continue his/her
journey to the Lord; they become channels of communication
through which the voice of God can echo within.

Regarding these, however, it must be emphasized that we are
not to insist that our "signpost" be identical to another's on

his/her journey to the Lord. Although a particular experience of God's presence and/or leading might be very helpful to us, it may not be the experience God is using to direct someone else. For example: Though you are moved to use every Wednesday and Friday as fast days, it does not follow that everyone who is journeying to the Lord must do the same. Or, if you find that a particular penance brings you a deeper awareness of God's presence, it does not mean that an identical penance will be the same avenue of grace for another. God's hold on us is far more individualized, depending on our need.

It is during this time of purgation that we begin accepting the reality of our sonship and daughtership, the fact of God's love, and the fact of our incomplete response. It is not meant to be a time of guilt or scruples, but a time for acknowledging our need for God's mercy, and accepting the mercy offered to us in Jesus. Such mercy, however, automatically calls us back to a deeper conversion response as the first darkness is approached.

## Darkness

Our "entrance" into the third stage of spiritual growth takes us through the first darkness noted on the diagram. It is here that the consolations and rewards which had been a source of encouragement for us are now absent. God, in a sense, now asks us to love not the "consolation of God" but the "God of consolation."

This is a difficult time for novices who wonder where God has gone. At first they immediately assume something is wrong: prayer is dry, there are no inner affective movements of grace, a cloud, blocking their vision of the Lord, seems to surround them.

This darkness is often described in terms of a desert, for there remains an inexplicable "thirsting" for the Lord, like the parched land thirsting for water. Although prayer and Eucharist and consolation seem to have little effect upon the individual, the "thirsting" continues and intensifies, making one very uncomfortable until the thirst is satisfied through the living water of the Spirit. This period of darkness, however, is very important if the sojourner is to savor the fruit of illumination and contemplation which usually follows.

During this transition period we also become more conscious of our sinfulness. Such self-awareness is important provided we respond correctly, not allowing our awareness of sin to keep us from continuing the journey, or receiving all that God offers. For it is here, in this awareness of personal sinfulness, when we are tempted to believe that we are not worthy of God's love, and could never be acceptable to God. The Evil One tries to convince us that anything and everything we do is for naught: that we are simply wasting our time.

The proper response to this temptation is faithfulness, not to what we see (our sinfulness) but to what we believe (our sonship and daughtership freely given to us by the Father in Jesus). We are called to remain faithful in prayer, realizing that feelings and affective responses are not what the Lord is seeking, but rather, "a heart contrite and pure" which will never be spurned.

Prayer, therefore, though dry, should be continued, remembering that every time we choose to pray we choose also to believe we are children of the Father. It is a time to reject the lies of the Evil One, who emphasizes our unworthiness, and to believe the scripture which reminds us:

> When the kindness and love of God our savior for mankind were revealed, it was not because he was concerned with any righteous actions we might have done ourselves; it was for no reason except his own

compassion that he saved us, by means of the cleansing water of rebirth and by renewing us with the Holy
Spirit which he has so generously poured over us
through Jesus Christ our Savior. He did this so that
we should be justified by his grace, to become heirs
looking forward to inheriting eternal life. (Tt. 3:4–8)

## Illumination/Contemplation

The most important thing to note about this stage is that
peace and freedom have gone above fear and anxiety, though
there are times when this might be experienced in the first two
stages. However, a person in the Illumination/Contemplation
stage experiences peace and freedom more often than not. This
should not be interpreted as a sign that "I've made it!" but that
the individual, blessed with God's gift of sonship/daugh-
tership, has begun to believe more deeply and completely that it
is so.

This stage also brings with it a heightened perception of reality. We begin to see things as they really are—gifts of the Father, offered to us through Jesus his Son, in the power of the
Spirit. One should not assume that this involves intense emo-
tion, or sheer willpower. On the contrary, the emotions and the
will are now being integrated and balanced, drawing us to
wholeness.

During this time we also find ourselves reviewing our lives,
remembering the gift that always was, namely, God's love, present with us from the beginning. This, of course, gives us cause
to celebrate and rejoice, realizing we have never been aban-
doned; we have always been his children.

It is here that the sacraments begin to take on a deeper meaning. They are seen as celebrations of the reality that is, rather than a means of obtaining that reality. In addition, sacramental power is seen as extending into all creation, thereby revealing its participation in the Divine reality. All that God has made is now seen as communicating his presence. Nature becomes alive; good is seen everywhere.

The sacraments of Penance and Eucharist also reveal their deeper meaning. Seen as a rich resource from which spiritual food and nourishment can be obtained, they are savored and celebrated with greater frequency than before. This occurs as the individual goes beyond the externals and perceives the deeper reality which the symbols are meant to illuminate.

What then is experienced at this time? More than likely, we begin to taste in some degree the truths we had accepted by faith, and acted upon in the purgative stage. In other words, we begin to know in the depth of our being that the Lord is risen. This knowledge, however, goes beyond any "reasons" which convince us. Now we know, in the biblical sense of the word, that by which we live and move and have our being. It is not just the mind or the heart which is involved, but our entire being, grasped by the reality of Jesus's Lordship. This "apprehension" by God, now directs us interiorly so we might move beyond doing gentle and peaceful things, and move toward being gentle and peaceful persons.

The process seduces us to detach ourselves from the need to receive rewards (consolations). Then, growing in detachment, we move toward the realization and acceptance that he who gives all is worthy of love, regardless of any benefit to ourselves. In a sense we begin to apprehend the awesome reality of God, realizing that love is within, and that our very identity stems from this love.

It is through this latter understanding that our love for others increases. We now can see why loving our neighbor, our enemy, or ourselves involves more than doing something for God. We are called to love because it is our nature to love. Love itself is at our center. To move away from love is to be unfaithful, not just to God, but to our very self-identity, our very definition. This is why we experience peace and restfulness more frequently: We have come to believe and accept our real identity from the Love centered within, rather than being centered on external achievements we may have accomplished.

As in the previous stages, Illumination/Contemplation is not a neat package identifiable in any one particular instance in our life. We have described it here so we can recognize the action of the Spirit in our lives, as we journey through all the stages, carrying, to some degree, each preceding one with us.

The person in the Illumination/Contemplation stage, therefore, is not a sinless person. Being more convinced that sonship/daughtership has been given, he/she has merely begun to live accordingly. It is from this reality that peace and freedom stem, not the doing of things, the accomplishment of tasks, or the performance of certain rituals.

Most Christians who are faithful to prayer, and to the Gospel of the Lord, will probably abide in this stage. Consciously accepting that they are children of the Father, they now can live in and with peace and freedom. This is the norm, not the extraordinary; it is meant for all believers in Jesus, not just for a special few.

## Darkness

This darkness is not the same as the first one described. Now the saint, stripped of defense mechanisms, vulnerable to all that the Lord offers, comes before God and realizes that everything that was done for God was really done for selfish reasons. It is the time when the individual presents his/her basket of accomplishments and successes to the Lord, only to discover it is empty.

Now the grace of trust is needed. The saint is asked to trust that, even though he/she has nothing to offer, the Lord accepts him/her; even though he/she has nothing to give in return for love, the Lord continues to offer unconditionally the gift of sonship/daughtership.

This is truly a difficult and dark time: a time of excruciating self-awareness, bringing the saint to the realization that his/her best motive was really self-centered; that the good works done were done for self, rather than for God; that the penances, prayers, mortification, and asceticism were done for selfish reasons rather than for the Lord who gives all.

This is not to say that the saint was "wrong" or "evil" in intent all these years! Rather, it simply points out how limited and empty our gifts are compared to the infinite gift of love itself. This darkness does not negate the good done, but shows it in the light of Good itself where everything looks pale.

Understanding this stage helps to explain why the saint continually repents of sinfulness, even though, in the eyes of the world, there does not seem to be any sin present. It is not that he/she is guilt-ridden, or overly scrupulous. It simply points to the deep awareness the individual has of the Light which is brighter than any other. As the mystic says, "When the light becomes brighter, the shadows become more distinct."

## Union

In this final stage the saint's delight is to see God's will done with no regard for personal pleasure or wants. Having died to self, the saint now accepts that he/she is nothing in God's presence, yet everything in his love, and desires now to conform to God's will that everything and everyone exist for him alone. Some would say that this experience is possible in this life; others that we taste it now, but it exists most completely after the resurrection.

Regardless of when this might take place, those who have approached this stage find themselves speechless before the awesome reality of the Almighty. They rely on poetry, contradicting images, or total silence in order to describe their experience. St. Thomas of Aquinas, for example, having experienced the power of God in this stage, declared that all his words were mere straw. He never wrote again, but lapsed into silent wonder until his death. St. Francis of Assisi, convinced in the depth of his being that all were in God, saw and experienced such unity and singularity in creation that he called them brothers and sisters. Nothing was "inanimate" to him; everything was alive with God.

This stage, therefore, seems to involve a new form of consciousness which literally breaks us free of our body's limitations, as a conscious, continual relationship with the Personal Absolute, revealed in Christ crucified, emerges. The heart is now set on the Changeless One who is a living, personal object of love, never an object of exploration. The reality of all that is, is now seen and accepted as the saint's reality also.

The person in this stage, therefore, returns to the world without being dominated by it. He/she is not a "superspiritual" freak, but an earthy, real, active, and alive person rooted in the world and able to change it. Hence, a Francis of Assisi can be called the saint of the topsy-turvy, not because he is out of the mainstream of life, but because in his life he revealed to the world precisely where the mainstream flowed.

Through all of this one must remember that no one stage is set and/or final at any one time. The different stages flow one into another, although the characteristics of one stage may predominate during a particular period of a person's life.

# APPENDIX B

## *Examples of Scripture Prayer*

### *Example One*

For our first example we will use the Transfiguration passage printed below. Begin by setting yourself in a relaxed position: comfortably upright, feet on the floor, regular breathing. Now thank the Father for the time you are about to spend with him. Ask him to send you the Spirit of Jesus so you might know and believe more completely the depth of his love. Ask always for a specific grace, especially the grace of loving the Lord more faithfully. Now read the chosen passage. Go slowly and prayerfully; there's no rush. Remember this is our food—it deserves more than a moment; it is our link with reality keeping our fragmented lives together, providing us with an inner unity and peace. Savor what is provided.

> Six days later, Jesus took with him Peter and James and his brother John and led them up a high mountain where they could be alone. There in their presence he was transfigured: his face shone like the sun and his clothes became as white as the light. Suddenly Moses and Elijah appeared to them; they were talking with him. Then Peter spoke to Jesus: "Lord," he said, "it is wonderful for us to be here; if you wish, I will make three tents here, one for you, one for Moses and one for Elijah." He was still speaking when suddenly a bright cloud covered them with a shadow, and from the cloud there came a voice which said, "This is my Son, the Beloved; he enjoys my favor. Listen to him." When they heard this, the disciples fell on their faces,

overcome with fear. But Jesus came up and touched
them. "Stand up," he said "do not be afraid." And
when they raised their eyes they saw no one but only
Jesus. (Mt. 17:1–8).

Having read the passage twice, sit quietly, close your eyes,
and allow your imagination to move you along.

See yourself walking along a dusty road. You are by yourself.
Suddenly, ahead of you, a small group of men appears from a
crossroad. You recognize them as Jesus with his companions,
Peter, James, and John. You run to them, asking if you may
walk with them. Jesus smiles as he says, "Come, follow."

You look toward the mountain ahead. It seems a long way
off. Jesus looks at you with great understanding. He knows your
fear: your fear of not staying with him on the journey; your fear
of giving up before the summit is reached. He calms you with
his gaze. Look into his eyes. What do you see? Bask in his gaze;
know that love holds you fast.

From a distance the mountain looks so imposing. Rising high
above the plain, it seems insurmountable. Tell that to Jesus. Tell
him that the roads crisscrossing the face of the mountain like
wrinkles on the face of a stranger frighten you. Yet you know
that you want to go on. Tell him so.

As you walk, hear Jesus speaking to his disciples about their
mission, and their need to remain faithful. Suddenly Jesus
speaks to you, explaining that he wants you to respond to his
invitation of union. The words are heard, but they don't register
in your mind. Ask him again to repeat what he said. Listen
carefully now.

Looking around you notice the beautiful flowers surrounding
the base of the mountain. They seem to lift their petals in
prayerful praise for the beauty which surrounds them. Jesus
begins to speak, so you move a bit closer: "Even Solomon in all
his glory was not arrayed as one of these. Yet you, my friends,

are far more important to my Father in heaven." He turns now to his disciples and continues to speak. You run to his side so you can hear every word. What is he saying?

As you walk up the mountain, Jesus takes your hand. He draws you closer to himself and begins speaking to you about his Father. He shares with you his own prayer with the Father, explaining how he tells his Father everything; how he comes often to this very mountain to spend time with the One he loves.

You come to a shady spot halfway up the mountain. Jesus invites you and his disciples to spend a few moments resting, by resting in his Father's love. Do that now, for as long as you want; tell the Father about your cares, your joys, your day, your hopes. Jesus will not leave without you.

Finally the top is reached. Sinking to his knees, Jesus begins to pray. You do likewise. You hear him praying. What is he saying to the Father? You strain your ears to hear every word. Suddenly you are lifted up; a sense of peace and joy overpowers you. What is it? You see a cloud; there are people there: Elijah the Prophet; Moses the Lawgiver. Then a voice, gentle, but firm: "This is my Son, the Beloved; he enjoys my favor. Listen to him." You bow down in silent worship before the God present to you.

Now they are talking about his passion. What are they saying? They look toward you; Jesus smiles and loves you with his eyes. You want to turn away, but you don't. Will you trust the gaze of love you have just seen?

Suddenly all are gone: the cloud, the voice, Moses, Elijah. You are alone with the Lord. Even the disciples are beyond your gaze. You see only Jesus. He comes toward you; you stumble for words, your eyes are cast down. Your heart, however, is full. Say what your heart feels.

Jesus comes now and takes your hand. He says, "Stand up and do not be afraid." You rise. Silently you travel back down the mountain, pondering all that you saw.

Thank him now for all that you saw. Ask for a word, or a phrase, or a picture which will stay with you throughout the day. Promise him that you will recall that word often, treasuring it as his special gift. Pray now the Our Father.

## Example Two

As in the first example, begin by setting yourself in a relaxed position: comfortably upright, feet on the floor, regular breathing. Next, follow the simple format listed below. It is quite easy, requiring nothing more than a bit of discipline, and an openness of heart. We will again use the Transfiguration passage quoted in Example One.

1. Begin with a short opening prayer. This can be a spontaneous prayer, or a standard one such as, "Come, Holy Spirit, fill the hearts of your faithful, and kindle in them the fire of your love. Send forth your Spirit that we may be created and you shall renew the face of the earth."

2. Follow this opening prayer with a period of silence.

3. Having chosen a scripture passage (the Psalms are especially good for this type of prayer), read it aloud, so the Word may touch your sense of sight and sound. Follow this with a period of silence.

4. Now, reread the passage, pausing after each thought or complete sentence. During these moments of silence, let the Word sink into the very depth of your being. From that silence (which may be as long or as short as the Spirit leads) allow your heart to speak its prayer, aloud or silently. This prayer, of course, would spring from the way the Word of scripture just

read touched the depth of your being. Using the Transfiguration text already cited (Mt. 17:1–8) the prayer might go like this:

First thought is read aloud:
"Six days later, Jesus took with him Peter and James and his brother John . . ."

Silence. If desired, follow this with prayer:
Lord, I praise and thank you for the invitation to walk with you, as you journey to the Father. Taking me to the most secret places of your heart, you reveal such love that I am overwhelmed. I know I am not worthy of this great privilege, yet you offer it to me. Help me accept the invitation, and treasure it for the gift it is.

Second thought is read aloud:
". . . and led them up to a high mountain where they could be alone."

Silence/prayer:
I'm so afraid of "alone," Lord. I'm so afraid of being there with you alone. Afraid of what you might do or say or ask or be. Oh, I know I've told you how I want to follow you, but the mountain seems so high right now. And we'd be alone. Just you and me.

Why this fear? Why this anxiety? You who are Love beckon me to the center of life, yet I'm afraid. Help me, Lord, with my fear of being alone with you.

Help me with my fear of you.

Next thought is read aloud:

"There in their presence he was transfigured: his face shone like the sun and his clothes became as white as the light."

Silence/prayer:

Lord, your glory is everywhere. I thank you for showing it to me this morning in the sun shining on the snowbanks; and in that man who played Santa Claus in front of the store. I thank you for revealing it to me in the Eucharist this morning. Thank you, Lord, for the brilliance of all creation that is your glory.

Next thought is read aloud:

"Suddenly Moses and Elijah appeared to them: they were talking with him."

Silence/prayer:

N.B. There is no "rule" which says that a prayer must be said aloud. Perhaps you will want to remain silent, savoring the word within. Perhaps a vocal prayer after each phrase gets in the way of your communion with the Lord. Should that be the case, say nothing; remain in silence after the section is read.

In addition, do not feel that an entire passage needs to be prayed through. The Lord might keep you on a phrase or a word for a long period of time. This is quite acceptable. Stay with the grace when and where the grace is given. Should you receive consolation and joy in the wordless pondering of the text, remain with the text. Do not move ahead.

Continue in similar fashion. When your prayer time is completed, end with a prayer of thanksgiving, perhaps the Our Father.

# APPENDIX C

## *Where Do I Find . . . ?*

This appendix is offered as a tool for the reader to help him/her locate familiar scripture stories. It is by no means a complete listing, although some have been cited in the meditations I have shared.

### *Old Testament*

## New Testament

The Baptism of Jesus

Mt. 3:13–17;
   Mk. 1:9–11
   Lk. 3:21–22

The Beatitudes
Born Again (Nicodemus)
Bread of Life
Brotherly Correction

Mt. 5:1–12
Jn. 3:1–21
Jn. 6:22–66
Mt. 18:15–18;
   Lk. 17:3

The Centurion's Servant

Mt. 8:5–13;
   Lk. 7:1–10;
   Jn. 4:46–53

The Children Come to Jesus

Mt. 19:13–15;
   Lk. 18:15–17;
   Mk. 10:13–16

The Christmas Story
The Commission

Mt. 1–2; Lk. 1–2
Mt. 28:19–20;
   Mk. 16:15

The Conversion of Saul

Ac. 9:1–19;
   22:5–16;
   26:10–18;

The Crucifixion, Death, and
   Resurrection

Mt. 26–28;
   Mk. 14:16;
   Lk. 22–24;
   Jn. 18–21

The Danger of Riches
The Early Christian Community

Mt. 19:23–26
Ac. 2:37–41;
   4:32–35

Emmaus, Road to
The End Times

Lk. 24:13–35
Mt. 24:26–44;
   Mk. 13; Lk. 21

Enter Through the Narrow Gate
Faith and Good Works
The Gentiles are Baptized

Mt. 7:13–14
Jm. 2:14–17
Ac. 10

| | |
|---|---|
| The Widow's Mite | Mk. 12:41–44; Lk. 21:1–4 |
| The Woman at the Well | Jn. 4:1–42 |
| Zacchaeus | Lk. 19:1–10 |

# APPENDIX D

## *The Books of the Bible in Alphabetical Order of Abbreviation*

| | | | |
|---|---|---|---|
| Ac. | Acts | Jm. | James |
| Am. | Amos | Jn. | John |
| Ba. | Baruch | 1 Jn. | 1 John |
| 1 Ch. | 1 Chronicles | 2 Jn. | 2 John |
| 2 Ch. | 2 Chronicles | 3 Jn. | 3 John |
| 1 Co. | 1 Corinthians | Jon. | Jonah |
| 2 Co. | 2 Corinthians | Jos. | Joshua |
| Col. | Colossians | Jr. | Jeremiah |
| Dn. | Daniel | Jude | Jude |
| Dt. | Deuteronomy | 1 Kg. | 1 Kings |
| Ep. | Ephesians | 2 Kg. | 2 Kings |
| Est. | Esther | Lk. | Luke |
| Ex. | Exodus | Lm. | Lamentations |
| Ez. | Ezekiel | Lv. | Leviticus |
| Ezr. | Ezra | 1 M. | 1 Maccabees |
| Ga. | Galatians | 2 M. | 2 Maccabees |
| Gn. | Genesis | Mi. | Micah |
| Hab. | Habakkuk | Mk. | Mark |
| Heb. | Hebrews | Ml. | Malachi |
| Hg. | Haggai | Mt. | Matthew |
| Ho. | Hosea | Na. | Nahum |
| Is. | Isaiah | Nb. | Numbers |
| Jb. | Job | Ne. | Nehemiah |
| Jdt. | Judith | Ob. | Obadiah |
| Jg. | Judges | 1 Pt. | 1 Peter |
| Jl. | Joel | 2 Pt. | 2 Peter |

| | | | |
|-----|---------------|-------|-----------------|
| Ph. | Philippians | Si. | Ecclesiasticus |
| Phm. | Philemon | Tb. | Tobit |
| Pr. | Proverbs | 1 Th. | 1 Thessalonians |
| Ps. | Psalms | 2 Th. | 2 Thessalonians |
| Qo. | Ecclesiastes | 1 Tm. | 1 Timothy |
| Rm. | Romans | 2 Tm. | 2 Timothy |
| Rt. | Ruth | Tt. | Titus |
| Rv. | Revelation | Ws. | Wisdom |
| 1 Sm. | 1 Samuel | Zc. | Zechariah |
| 2 Sm. | 2 Samuel | Zp. | Zephaniah |
| Sg. | Song of Songs | | |

## ABOUT THE AUTHOR

FATHER CHRISTOPHER ARIDAS has written several articles on parish ministry for the Paulist magazine *Catholic Charismatic* as well as two other books, *Discernment: Seeking God In Every Situation,* and *Your Catholic Wedding.* In addition, he has had several original compositions of liturgical music published and recorded. He serves as the Bishop's Liaison for the Charismatic Renewal in the diocese of Rockville Centre (Long Island). He holds degrees in English and Philosophy, as well as a Master of Divinity in Theology.

# OTHER IMAGE BOOKS

AGING: THE FULFILLMENT OF LIFE – Henri J. M. Nouwen and Walter J. Gaffney

AN AQUINAS READER – Ed., with an Intro., by Mary T. Clark

BATTLE FOR THE AMERICAN CHURCH – Msgr. George A. Kelly

BIRTH OF THE MESSIAH – Raymond E. Brown

THE BISHOPS AND THE BOMB – Jim Castelli

BREAKTHROUGH: MEISTER ECKHART'S CREATION SPIRITUALITY IN NEW TRANSLATION – Matthew Fox

CATHOLIC AMERICA – John Cogley

CHRISTIAN LIFE PATTERNS – Evelyn and James Whitehead

THE CHURCH – Hans Küng

CITY OF GOD – St. Augustine – Ed. by Vernon J. Bourke. Intro. by Étienne Gilson

COMPASSION – Donald P. McNeill, Douglas A. Morrison, Henri J. M. Nouwen

A CONCISE HISTORY OF THE CATHOLIC CHURCH (Revised Edition) – Thomas Bokenkotter

THE CONFESSIONS OF ST. AUGUSTINE – Trans., with an Intro., by John K. Ryan

CONJECTURES OF A GUILTY BYSTANDER – Thomas Merton

CONTEMPLATION IN A WORLD OF ACTION – Thomas Merton

CONTEMPLATIVE PRAYER – Thomas Merton

CREATIVE MINISTRY – Henri J. M. Nouwen

A CRY FOR MERCY – Henri J. M. Nouwen

DARK NIGHT OF THE SOUL – St. John of the Cross. Ed. and trans. by E. Allison Peers

DAWN WITHOUT DARKNESS – Anthony T. Padovano

DOORS TO THE SACRED: A HISTORICAL INTRODUCTION TO SACRAMENTS IN THE CATHOLIC CHURCH – Joseph Martos

EVERLASTING MAN – G. K. Chesterton

THE FREEDOM OF SEXUAL LOVE – Joseph and Lois Bird

GENESEE DIARY – Henri J. M. Nouwen

THE HERMITAGE JOURNALS – John Howard Griffin

A HISTORY OF PHILOSOPHY: VOLUME 1 – GREECE AND ROME (2 Parts) – Frederick Copleston, S.J.

A HISTORY OF PHILOSOPHY: VOLUME 2 – MEDIAEVAL PHILOSOPHY (2 Parts) – Frederick Copleston, S.J. Part I – Augustine to Bonaventure. Part II – Albert the Great to Duns Scotus

# OTHER IMAGE BOOKS

# OTHER IMAGE BOOKS

# OTHER IMAGE BOOKS

B 84 – 4